*How to Leave Home
— and Make Everybody Like It*

Other Books by the Author

Pasteur and the Invisible Giants

Legal Action: A Layman's Guide

Amnesty: The American Puzzle

A Lion in the Sun: The Rise and Fall of the British Empire

Disaster 1906: The San Francisco Earthquake and Fire

What You Can Do About Your Headaches

Inventors for Medicine

The Complete Beginner's Guide to Bowling

The Complete Beginner's Guide to Making and Flying Kites

Basic Football Strategy

How to Leave Home —and Make Everybody Like It

EDWARD F. DOLAN, Jr.

DODD, MEAD & COMPANY
NEW YORK

2 3 4 5 6 7 8 9 10

Library of Congress Cataloging in Publication Data

Dolan, Edward F   date
    How to leave home—and make everybody like it.

    SUMMARY: A guide to leaving home and living
independently including breaking the news to the family,
finding a job, the pros and cons of running away, and
handling personal finances.
    1. Youth—United States. 2. Youth—Conduct of
life. 3. Finance, Personal. 4. Runaway youth—
United States. [1. Youth—Conduct of life. 2. Finance, Personal. 3. Runaways] I. Title.
HQ796.D58   158′.2   77-6500
ISBN 0-396-07475-8

This book is for
William Royse,
for his help in its preparation
and for thirty years worth
of good talk and friendship

Acknowledgments

I am indebted to many people for their assistance in the preparation of this book. First, my appreciation must go to William Royse, whose many years in counseling and whose long and patient discussions with me contributed so much to the shape and direction of the book, and to fellow writer Richard B. Lyttle for all his encouragement and sound editorial comment.

A special word of thanks is due the good friends who answered all those individual questions that had to be asked along the way: James B. Soetaert, Chief Deputy Probation Officer, Marin County, California; Jack Blaine, Juvenile Commissioner, Marin County, California; Paul Mobley, Assistant Superintendent, Novato Unified School District, California; Frederick J. Hass, M.D.; independent insurance agent C. Paul Bettini; attorney Robert Bennet Mc-Creadie; and Douglas W. Brown and Mrs. Greta De-Graves, both of Crocker National Bank, California.

I owe a particular debt to the more than fifty young

people who contributed their advice and the stories of their own first days of independence. Because of the personal nature of their experiences, they are identified by their first names only throughout the book.

The quotations in Chapter 4 are from a copyrighted article, "More Kids on the Road—Now It's the Throwaways," which appeared in the May 12, 1975, issue of *U.S. News & World Report*.

Contents

Finding a Job — Job Sources — Looking for a Job —
Your Resumé and Letter of Application — The Job
Interview

You and Your Roommate — Picking the Right Room-
mate — Your Invaluable Health — Health and Dis-
ability Insurance — Finding Medical Help and a
Doctor — For the Future: Marriage — Marriage and
Freedom — The Age for Marriage — For the Future:
Education — If You're Going to College — Junior Col-
leges — Technical and Correspondence Schools —
That All-Important High School Diploma

1

Time to Go

Your whole life lies ahead, but you know that you must leave home before you can get to it. Perhaps you want to find a job across town or across the country. Perhaps attend a distant college or technical school. Head around the world to all the places where the action is. Rent an apartment, by yourself, with a friend, or a loved one. Marry. Things are great between you and your parents, but nothing's going to start for you until you leave home.

Or perhaps you're just the opposite. You want to go because you can't stand your parents any more. You don't get along at all. You're always fighting. They don't seem to understand you. Maybe they don't even seem to like you.

Or maybe you're somewhere in between. You don't dislike your folks and you've got no big plans for the future. It's just that you seem to be suffocating around the house. Maybe you've done one household chore too many. Maybe school is getting you down. Maybe you're tired of being watched as you come and go. Maybe you just want that great feeling of standing on your own two feet and being your own boss.

Whatever your reasons and whatever your feelings for your parents, you know that the day for leaving home is coming fast. You can't wait for it to get here.

But—

It's no fun to think of what lies between your first days of independence and where you stand now. You're going to have to get out the front door. You're pretty certain there will be trouble with your parents. If yours is a close-knit family, they may be wounded to know that you no longer wish to live with them. If you're without plans for the future, they'll undoubtedly worry about what you're going to do with yourself. If you're still a bit underage, they may forbid you to go, and then—as is their right—come after you if you do leave. And if you're always battling, this could be the worst fight yet.

You may not only be worried about your parents. You may have a few worries about yourself. What's going to happen to your resolve if your mother cries? If your father asks a lot of questions about the future that you can't answer? If everyone tries to yell you down and forbids you to leave? Or if you yourself, when the rosy dream of leaving becomes a reality, begin to wonder if you can really hack life on your own?

With all this in mind, you're steeling yourself to face not only your parents but yourself. You're primed for an argument. You're determined to admit no fear and to show no weakness in your resolve to go. You've promised yourself to win at all costs. You're sure that everyone, yourself included, is going to be hurt before you're safely away. Indeed, it's no fun to think about.

But You're Not Alone

If it's any comfort, you're not alone in your feelings and never have been. Millions of today's young people share them; just listen to your friends become prophets of doom when they begin talking about cutting loose. And countless of the young people who have gone before you through the centuries have had to endure them when the time for independence was at hand. They're among the most human of emotions. And among the worst to deal with. They can make the departure from home not what it should be—a glorious testing of young wings—but a problem full of worry, tears, and harsh words.

The fact that leaving home can be such a problem is one of life's oddities. After all, the desire to fly free and live an independent life has always been natural and traditional in the young. As one psychologist puts it:

"Since the beginning of time, young people have been moving out of the nest and setting up places of their own and then standing aside years later while their kids have done the same thing. If we weren't meant to operate this way, if we were intended to always live in our parents' house, then all of mankind would still be lumped together under one big roof. But new homes for each new generation—that's the way we human beings do things. You'd think we'd be used to it by now."

Some families are. While still communicating their love, the parents gracefully stand aside, and sometimes help the kids along. The children leave easily, without thinking that they're abandoning or insulting anyone. Everyone seems to realize that independence is the expected and desired thing.

But for too many other families—perhaps *most* families, some psychologists say—the apron strings can only be cut with pain, sometimes anguish.

Why?

Some Answers

For some of the answers, you need only look at what's going on today. Your generation is marrying younger than has been the case in years. You may be sure that you're ready for marriage, but your parents may wonder if you've got the maturity for it. If a wedding isn't planned, then more of you than ever are taking off to live together. This may seem perfectly natural to you, but your parents, raised in a different moral climate, may be deeply shocked. And, while each new generation has always challenged the values of the one that went before it, the cry against the way things were is at its loudest today. You may see society as money-grubbing and computerized and want the simple life, growing your own food and practicing an Eastern religion, but your parents may see you as wandering aimlessly into the sunset, without a chance of doing a thing with your life once you finally wake up.

As if all this isn't enough, you live in a mobile society. There was a time when most young Americans packed up and moved across town (and it was usually a small town) or settled on the farm just down the road. Now the move from home is likely to take you to a job clear across the country. You look up from your packing and see in your parents the aching knowledge that the future holds only long-distance calls and a visit now and again. Suddenly, you feel guilty. And, just as suddenly, there can be anything from stiff-lipped silence to tears to angry words.

And let's not forget the "generation gap" that books, magazines, films, and television programs love to talk about. You've heard everything that's being said—how your parents don't understand you, your values, your clothes, your language, your music; how they don't trust your judgment, don't appreciate your motives, and won't be happy until they've molded you in their own image. The result can be a certainty on your part that they'll fight to hold you and save you from a life they find incomprehensible and perhaps even dangerous. You're just as determined to fight for the way you want to live.

What's Going On Inside

But these are all outside influences. We also have to put up with some inner problems. Perhaps the worst of the lot is the problem of breaking a years-long habit.

We humans remain with our parents longer than is the case with any other animal. The habit of being with them is firmly entrenched. And, since we're reasoning creatures, this attachment is more than instinctual. We've defined it and given it a name—love. It is compounded of many factors—the dependence that we once felt on our parents, the sacrifices that we know (or have been told) they made for us, the care they gave us, and that core-of-being understanding that we are of and a part of them.

And so the time comes to leave. No matter how eager we are to go, no matter how tired we are of being babied or bossed, no matter that we may spend most of the time fighting, there is still a part of us that's in turmoil. We can't help the feeling. We're breaking an old habit. We're altering an old pattern of love, even if we seem to feel no love at the time. A sense of guilt comes quickly.

Emotions being the tangled things they are, it's a guilt that can just as quickly become an anger directed against the very ones we feel guilty about. A young friend of mine, now twenty-six, says it all when he remembers:

"I was mad as hell and I really didn't know why. It wasn't until about two, three years later that I figured it out. I was using my anger to cover up my feelings about thinking I was hurting my people. I was justifying what I was doing to them—or what I thought I was doing."

He admits that his anger made no sense, for "my people really offered no resistance. In fact, I think my dad thought it was high time I was on my own."

He was lucky. His people weren't possessive. But some parents are. They can't bear to lose you and the way things have been for so long. Now there are looks of pain or too obvious efforts to hide them. Now there may be pleas or even bribes to keep you in the house. Your anger grows, helped along by a very real threat—the threat of being kept a prisoner without chains.

There's another side to the habit problem. Throughout childhood, we're subject to parental authority. No one would argue that it isn't necessary to guide us past the dangers of the early years. But, even when we're beyond the "don't touch that" or "no, you can't stay out past ten" stages, the memory of it lingers. When the time comes to leave, the young person may expect to run into it when it's not really there, and then speak unwisely, hurtfully. Or the parent, perhaps without really thinking, may try to use it. In either case, there's trouble.

To make matters worse, an outside influence often gets mixed up in things about now. We live in a time when young people everywhere are fighting authority, sometimes justifiably, sometimes not. Our institutions are under fire. Our political leaders are viewed with open suspicion. The double standard—one for the wealthy and one for the poor, one for whites and one for minorities—is under attack. In such an age, it becomes easy to see all authority, even the best and necessary, as vicious, domineering, and resistant to every effort to be free of it.

And easy for that attitude to filter down to the family level. Parents have represented a basic authority that we've known since birth. Further, they may seem to be a part of that outside oppression that seems so dangerous. So, often without bothering to check how they really feel, we face them with hostility and defiance. And, at times, we meet parents who *are* oppressive. Again, in either case, there's trouble.

Does It Have to Be This Way?

All these influences—external and internal—are making what has always been a difficult time for many families more difficult than ever before. In some families, it has turned it into a completely shattering experience. It's hard enough to leave home in the best of circumstances. There are bound to be spoken or secret regrets on all sides. A family unit that has been together for years is breaking up. Long-established relationships are changing. Life will never again be as it was. But, when all the external and internal forces are at work, the regrets can be sharper, the words harsher, and the tears hotter. And, if there is bitterness between parent and child, it can ferment into acid.

But does it have to be this way for you?

The fact is, it needn't be. There will be regrets at your departure, yes, and perhaps some bitterness. But you can keep both at a minimum and even erase the bitterness altogether. You can get out the front door without slamming it, without leaving behind words that have cut and will take years to forget. Instead of breaking up the family unit, you can leave in such a way as to create a whole series of new and healthy relationships with your loved ones.

That is, if you use your head.

And that is the purpose of this book—to talk about using your head. To talk about picking the best time to leave. To talk about saying and doing the right things, the kind things, when you break the news of your intentions. To talk about getting yourself into the fittest shape possible for departure so that you can answer any parental concerns or objections. And to talk about intelligently handling all the problems and responsibilities that go with independence.

Actually, by reading this far, you've already made a start. At least, you've looked your feelings straight in the face, whether they be regret, guilt, anger, or just a general nervousness. At least, you've seen some of the outside forces that can creep into the house to worsen matters. And some of the internal forces that can get in your way.

Seeing these things and understanding that they're quite commonplace and have touched millions of other young people, you needn't now be their victim. They're not peculiar to you and so you don't have to worry that something's wrong with you because they're in your life. Nor worry that you're powerless to do something about them. You can begin to control them. With control comes the freedom to use your head.

Now let's put the head to work. Let's see what you can do with it when, as you should, you sit down with your parents and take the time to say:

"Mom. Dad. I want a life of my own."

2

Five Steps to Independence

"When can I leave?"

This question—which really means "When can I leave *legally*, so that my parents can't come after me?"—is always among the first to be asked when the subject of departing home comes up. In general, there are three answers. So that you'll know the right time to talk with your folks about a life of your own, let's get to the answers before we do anything else.

You may legally leave home:

1. When you reach the *age of majority*, the law's terms for adulthood. Many young people believe that adulthood comes at the voting age, which is now eighteen. This is not true, for the states are allowed to set their own ages of majority. The ages presently run from eighteen to twenty-one across the country, often with one for men and another for women. You'd best check to learn the age set by your state.

or

2. When you *marry*. You may marry at one age without your parents' consent and at a younger age with their consent. At a still younger age, you may not marry even with their permission. These ages are set by the individual states and vary from state to state. On page 151, you'll find a chart listing the ages for marriage state-by-state.

or

3. When you undergo a *change of guardianship*. This is a legal technicality that enables you to leave your natural home in the event of difficulty and go to the home of someone appointed as your guardian. You hold the same responsibilities to the guardian that you held to your parents and may not leave his home until you reach the age of majority, marry, or undergo yet another change of guardianship. Since all this is a legal technicality that may never apply in your case, it's mentioned here just to get it on the record.

Also, if you're under the age of majority but of a responsible nature and earning your own living, you may leave home legally if you have your parent's permission. They, however, continue to be responsible for you and must take you back and/or provide support if you run into difficulty or are unable to go on earning your own living.

If you're now at or fast approaching the time to be legally independent, this chapter hopes to help you talk with your parents so that your departure will be made all the easier.

An Approach to Your Talk

I once heard Eldridge Cleaver tell an audience: "If you're not part of the solution, you're part of the problem."

He was talking about curing social and political ills, but his words hold an important key for your approach. Your departure is bound to be a problem for as long as your parents oppose it, even if you have the legal right to be on your way. But suppose that, when you approach them, you manage to present the problem as one they can help solve. They'll stop being a part of it as soon as they forget their worries for even a moment and make some contribution, no matter how small, to its solution. Suddenly, they'll be on your side.

A friend of mine recalls the turning point in her leave-home talk. It came when her mother said, "But have you thought of how you're going to cook? I'll bet you don't even have the money for pots and pans."

"You're just about right, Mom. But I was thinking. What about that old set Aunt Grace gave you? I mean, if you've got no use for it."

"Yes. It would get you by. And there are my old dishes. You could have them, too."

Right then, my friend remembers, she knew she was on her way. Mother had started to work on the solution. She'd broken through the barrier of her own resistance. Now it was only natural for her—as for anyone—to want to go on and solve the rest of the problem.

It may take a little time to get your mother (or father) to say something like this girl's mother said. But it's worth the wait. And well worth the effort to head in this direction right from the beginning.

As soon as you begin to talk with your parents, try to

set the feeling that you're putting your dream out on the table for them to see. Try to establish a mood that will make it easy for them to cooperate and come up with suggestions that make them a part of the solution. Let them know that you'd like their advice—and then don't be afraid or too proud to take it when you know it's good. Let them see that you're listening to what they say.

And, of course, don't just pretend. Actually listen. All sorts of trouble can be saved. For instance, perhaps you're still underage by a few weeks or months. Your parents are unwilling to see you go right now, but you hear them say that they'll be willing and even ready to help you along on your next birthday. Knowing this, you may be able to find the patience to wait. And you may be able to settle some of the problems that are behind your wanting to leave; they needn't now be a bother during the brief time you'll remain at home.

No one is saying that it's easy to establish the proper mood. You may run into trouble along the way. Your parents may be shocked at your news. Perhaps hurt. There may be tears. But, even then, the mood can still be set. Just take your time. Just try to be patient and understanding.

And try always to remember the following five points. Though they're all-important, there's nothing profound or magical about them. They're just common-sense ways of approaching people and helping them to see your side of things. I've seen them work and I've gotten in the habit of calling them the "Five Steps to Independence."

Step One: Don't Just Plunge In

Your talk is going to be one of the most important in your life. So, no matter how impatient you may be, don't just plunge in. Your chances for success will be much greater if you'll do two other things instead.

First, try to pick a good moment to begin. You can't hope to set a good mood if you've just had a fight with your parents, if Dad's grinding his teeth after a rotten day at the office, or if the family's favorite television program is on. Bide your time until the atmosphere seems right. If it seems wise or necessary, you might tell your folks ahead of time—say, just before dinner—that you'd like to talk to them after the dishes are done.

On the other hand, the right moment might crop up unexpectedly. Perhaps everyone is in a relaxed and happy mood after some good dinnertime conversation. Perhaps you've all been discussing some topic that's right next door to the one you have in mind. Watch for such moments and be ready to take advantage of them.

Second, prepare what you're going to say well ahead of time. Too much can't be said in favor of preparation. It can reduce much of your nervousness (although it probably won't get rid of it altogether) and can keep you from forgetting things you want to say or from saying things you don't want to say.

It's best, of course, to spend the preparation time by yourself, preferably in a quiet spot—your room or under your favorite tree on campus—without a radio going full blast. Think about *what* you're going to say, the *order* in which you're going to say it, and *how* you're going to say it. Imagine the questions and objections that you may encounter and then work out answers to them.

One all-important point: When thinking ahead to possible questions or objections, try not to let your imagination run away with you. Don't think that Dad is automatically going to fly into a rage, that Mother is going to wail, or that they're both going to lock you in your room and hide the key. If you let yourself think negatively, you run the risk of unconsciously making things turn out badly just to prove yourself right. So spend the time on the positive side, quietly thinking of how you can set the right mood and guide the conversation along the lines you want it to take.

Step Two: Say Your Say—Calmly

Even the most reasonable of parents can be blind to certain facts. Chiefly, they have the habit of thinking that their children are not as grown-up or as capable as perhaps is actually the case.

If you can curb your nervousness or your anger and speak calmly, you'll help your cause in two ways. You'll not only be setting the right mood but you'll also be demonstrating the chief characteristics necessary for successful independence—maturity and level-headedness. You'll be showing everyone that you're not the child of yesteryear. And helping everyone to forget those tantrums you threw at nine or the way you stormed out the back door when you couldn't have your way at fourteen or—let's face it— perhaps just the other day.

The idea of maturity is especially important if you're still a bit underage. If you're of legal age for independence, you can still depart and no one can stop you should your talk come to nothing. But if you're underage, your parents have every right to forbid you to leave. And so you'll need to prove a number of things to them—that you can earn your own living, care for yourself, maintain your own place, and give your life direction. All these things require a maturity on your part.

Show that maturity as you talk and your people may be proud and willing to help you along your way.

Even with maturity, however, you may find it hard to keep your temper and nervousness under control. Still, give it a real try, even if you feel pushed to the limit and even if you're hearing something about yourself that hurts. Anger and emotion can really trip you up if you let them get loose.

They can make you look sullen when you're trying to be serious as you answer some probing question or explain some difficult feeling. They can make you see every question as a challenge or an insult when, in reality, it may just be a request for information. They can make you lash out just to relieve the tension inside you when, in a few moments, a turn in the conversation might cause it to evaporate anyway.

Above all else, remember that anger and emotional turmoil are contagious. If you lose control, you can count on your upset spreading quickly to your parents. But, if you remain calm, you'll insure their calmness. And, should their emotions start to rise at any point, your manner will likely calm them before things get out of hand.

Step Three: Say Your Say—with Kindness

If you speak with friendly calm, kindness will almost automatically be there. But, to be certain, make a conscious effort for it just the same. By itself, it's the best thing you've got for setting the right mood. More important—especially if you've been having trouble with your parents—it can keep you away from those remarks, so often thoughtless, that may ruin everything in an instant and hurt for years to come.

Try always to avoid being harsh and critical. Don't harp on those little things that have always annoyed you. If you hear something about yourself that you don't like, forget about replying in kind. When explaining your reasons for leaving, go so far as to tell your parents that it's not because you can't stand their life-style or their politics any longer, but because you want your chance to try life on your own. Let them know that you love and admire them.

On some of these points, you may be stretching the truth a little. Go ahead and stretch it. Your pride or integrity won't really be hurt. The warm glow that you leave behind will far outweigh any damage. Also, it's a good idea to remember the old saying that the only constant thing in life is change. You might have the same experience as a young teacher now working in Seattle. He says:

"I almost choked when I told my folks that I really liked —I mean loved—them. Now I'm glad I did. I've changed my mind about them. That was five years ago, and you know what? I was actually expressing my true feelings."

There's one kindness that can be of particular help. Don't give the impression that you're disappearing, never to be seen again. If you're moving across town, tell your parents that you'll be dropping by, calling, or visiting regularly. Or having them over to your place. If you're going any distance, promise to write. Plan to exchange telephone calls. Think about coming home for a vacation as soon as your finances will permit.

And need it be said? Keep your promises.

Step Four: Have Something to Say

Before ever talking with your parents, develop a plan for what you'll do after you're gone. Assess yourself and your chances of making that plan work and then adjust it accordingly. Though this is the fourth step to be talked about, it's the first one that should be tackled. Its importance just can't be overemphasized. It can do three things for you.

First, of course, a plan will give you something definite to talk about. You'll find it easier to set the right mood and keep the conversation safely away from danger spots. You'll be better able to maintain your calm, answer questions, and overcome objections. And, if the plan is a solid one, you'll be better able to prove your maturity and put many—if not most—of your parents' worries to rest.

On this last point, Joe, now a copywriter with an advertising agency, recalls:

"I had just gotten into Columbia University and I wanted an apartment in town near the campus. My father didn't think the apartment was a good idea. He was all for me commuting from Connecticut so that I could save the rent money. But I had the answers all ready—about how I'd have extra time for study in the library, about how I wouldn't be so tired from traveling, about how I'd checked to make sure that my VA benefits and a part-time job I'd gotten would cover all my expenses. . . . The next thing I knew he was saying, 'Are you sure you can make it in this apartment, or maybe we can look for a cheaper one . . .' and suddenly I realized I had him on my side. The rest was a cinch."

Second, a plan may put your parents' worries to rest for yet another reason. Let's say that you're still a few months underage. Juvenile law in the United States is being changed constantly, but one rule seems to be holding fast throughout the country: parents can be held liable for the criminal acts of and the damage done by their underage children. Your people may well wonder if, when out from under their control, you're going to wreck an apartment, smash up a car, or break someone's nose in a fight. Much the same sort of thing can happen while you're still at home, of course, but the chances can be greater during the first heady days of freedom. With a solid plan, you may convince your parents that you're level-headed enough to get by on your own without doing something that can cost them a bundle. It's a feeling of safety to which they're entitled.

Third, and perhaps of greatest importance, only with a plan can you have a real chance to make your independence stick.

You may want to come home for visits. That's great. But who wants to end up back for good, suitcase in hand and egg all over your face, saying, "Is my old room still there?" If you're now thinking of nothing more than getting clear of the house, then it's worth listening to what so many young people who have gone the same route warn: You're in for a bad what-do-I-do-now time as soon as the front door closes behind you. It can be a confusing and discouraging time. It's broken many young people and has sent them home in defeat.

Incidentally, there's nothing shameful about a return home—and you should certainly come back if the circumstances so dictate. There's no use starving or risking trouble with the authorities if you find yourself wondering where your next meal is coming from. But there's nothing great about a return either. It's hard on both you and your parents.

For you, it's embarrassing. You feel like a failure. You keep seeing relatives with those "I told you so" looks on their faces. Inside, you may wonder if you'll ever be able to make it on your own. Before they're done, all these things can make your next departure twice as difficult as the first.

As for your parents, though they may loyally welcome you back, they're likely to be upset. Your departure caused them to make a major adjustment in their lives. Now, just when they've gotten used to not having you around, they've got to make another. Maybe the fact that they no longer had to finance your appetite has enabled them to think about buying new furniture or taking that long-dreamed-of vacation. Out the window go those plans. Maybe they've moved in the time you've been away, renting that compact, easy-to-keep apartment they've always wanted. Now, somehow, they're going to have to squeeze you in.

It's rough all around—on you and on them.

But, with a plan, you can avoid all the trouble. You can put yourself in the best position possible to make your independence last a lifetime.

The plan, however, has to be a good one. A set of half-baked notions about what you're going to do will get you nowhere. An intelligent parent can see through them as though they're a newly cleaned window.

Incidentally, if you're a young woman, your plan may have to be an especially good one. Your folks may be like those countless parents who, regardless of what's going on in the world, still feel that a daughter should remain under the family wing until she marries. They may even want you back in the house after you've been away to college for a few years and have survived quite nicely on your own. It's an old-fashioned idea, but it's still a long way from dying out completely and can be very troublesome.

Undoubtedly, you've already told them—probably time and again—that the role of woman is changing and that you're perfectly capable of taking your place in today's world and living successfully by yourself until you're ready to marry. If they've believed you at all, they've likely only half-believed you. A solid plan—and the display of determination and good sense behind it—may do much to erase the *half* from that belief.

To develop a solid plan, no matter your sex, you really should have a long talk with yourself. All bravado, impetuosity, and impatience should be set to one side. You should leave yourself free to look some cold facts squarely in the face. And free to ask and answer a whole string of questions:

1. Am I really old enough just yet to live alone?
2. Can I yet handle all the financial, social, and legal obligations that come with independence?
3. Will I be able to continue my education or my training for a job?
4. I've got a job now, but is it the one I want for the rest of my life? Where do I go from here? Will I get there if I'm on my own?
5. The place where I'll live—will I really be happy there?
6. The friend or loved one I'll live with—will we really be happy together in the long run? If I'm in love, is it really for a lifetime? Or am I just telling myself that?
7. The life-style I've chosen—deep down, do I really feel I'll be happy with it?
8. Have I got the money to support myself for any length of time?
9. All along, I've been telling myself that, whatever I do, everything will turn out all right. Will it? Honestly?

These questions and all the others that will come to mind are hard ones to ask. You may like the answers to some and hate the answers to others. Honest answers, though, will give you a look at yourself that perhaps you've never seen before.

If you then develop a plan on the basis of the answers and this new self-knowledge, you'll not only be on the right track for winning your parents' cooperation but also headed for that best independence of all—the one that's permanent.

Step Five: Try Again

While the first four steps give you your best chance to set the right mood and win your parents' cooperation, there's no guarantee you'll get that cooperation immediately. That's where step five comes in.

Your folks may be too shocked or upset to come over to your side in a matter of minutes or even hours. Or too possessive. They may need time to get over thinking of you as the child you are not. They may be the sort that needs time to think *anything* over.

This can be disappointing, discouraging, and maddening. But there's no need to blow up. No need to keep pushing your point as if you're a little kid begging for permission to stay overnight at a friend's house. No need to think that all is lost.

Instead, it's time to think about gently backing off for a little while. You're obviously not getting anywhere. But you may get all the cooperation you'll need just by giving everyone a chance to relax, cool down, and think. Then you can try again when the time is right.

But how long must you wait for the right time? Much will depend on how you and your folks are reacting to each other. Maybe you sense that a coffee break will do the trick. Maybe it's best to call it a night and say that everybody needs a little rest and that you'd like to talk some more tomorrow or the next day. When you meet again, you may find that things haven't improved enough. Then don't be afraid to leave the door open for still another talk.

A delay is probably the last thing you want. You may feel as if it's sending you straight up the walls. But try to think about the trouble it can save. It will give your parents time to get used to the idea of not having you around; maybe that's all that is needed. They may remember how they felt when they were young. If you're underage, they'll have a chance to talk things over and may agree that you're nevertheless mature enough for independence and should be given the chance. Or one parent may be secretly on your side and use the time to win the other over.

In one way or another, no matter how impatient you are, a "go slow" approach and a "cooling off" time can only work in your favor.

The "five steps to independence" can be worth all the effort and patience they will require of you. They can turn your departure into a cooperative family effort. Avoided can be the anger, hurt, and frustration that must come when you have to bang the door shut behind you and leave in defiance. The departure now can be a loving one—as can the future.

3

About Taking Off

It's fine to think about talking with your folks, winning their approval, and making your departure a loving one. It all sounds great. But what if you feel that you can't possibly approach your parents in the first place, much less convince them to see things your way?

Perhaps, as are thousands of today's young people, you're planning a life-style that can make even the most tolerant Mother and Dad turn pale. For instance, maybe you've got your eye on a commune. Perhaps you're going to practice an Eastern religion or join a sect such as the Moonies' Unification Church. It may be that you and a loved one have decided to set up housekeeping together without first saying "I do" in front of a clergyman or a judge.

Or your reluctance to talk may stem from some other problem. Perhaps you're living with a divorced or widowed parent. You may think that he or she will be unable to get along without your help around the house or your financial assistance. Or perhaps you feel that your parents' possessiveness or a lifetime of fighting with you promises to kill all talk before it starts.

Any of these difficulties—or any like them—may seem to leave you with only one avenue of escape if you're to be free. Talk is impossible and so you're just going to take off. You're going to leave without a word or come downstairs with your bags packed and tell everyone to get out of the way.

Regardless of your age, the decision just to take off can be a hard one. There's at least one problem you'll have to face if you're of a legal age for independence—and many young people have found it a big one. The problems, of course, are many if you're underage. You're setting yourself up to be chased as a runaway.

First, let's talk about taking off if you're legally old enough to do so. Then we'll turn to those many problems faced by the underage runaway.

If You're Old Enough

Once you've reached the age of majority, no one can stop you from leaving, and no one can come after you and force you to return. The law sees you as an adult. You're entitled to live independently.

And so the problem about taking off at the age of majority has nothing to do with the law. Rather, it has to do with the hurt and anger that you can leave behind and the sense of guilt you can heap on yourself for leaving them behind.

While preparing this book, I talked with a number of

young people who had "taken off." Most of them said that they had experienced these feelings, hadn't liked them, and hadn't felt right or really free until things were squared with the family. From the nods he got, one young man seemed to nail it down for everyone when he said, "Where's the fun of being on your own when you're up to your neck in a bag of guilts?"

Some had never gotten along at home. Still, they had found that they had no desire to hurt their people. As one said, "I wouldn't have called it love. Maybe it was, but so deep-seated that I couldn't see it. Or maybe it was an old loyalty. Whatever it was, it sure came to the surface."

A few hadn't cared what anyone felt at the time. They had just wanted to get away. Later, they changed their views. Betty was one of them. Now married, she recalled:

"I ran away several times when I was sixteen and seventeen after some terrible fights with my mother. The last time, I turned eighteen while I was crashing with a friend. My family got a private detective to find me, but I refused to go home, refused to talk to anybody, especially my mother.... For a long time, I didn't even think about her, and then it was Christmas and all of a sudden I was homesick—wow, homesick, get that!—and I was wanting to make things up with her. I couldn't believe it, but that's what I wanted. ... God, what I went through making up my mind to call home. ... Then all the two of us could do was cry and say we were sorry. ... Everything's fine with us now. ..."

Adding to the trouble can be a sense of disappointment in self. There were three young people who felt that if you're old enough to be on your own, you're also old enough to state your views to your parents, answer questions, face objections, and take the heat of criticism without going to pieces. If you can't face your parents, they wondered, how can you expect to face life?

There seems to be just one way to avoid these feelings altogether, or at least in part—and that's to talk over your plans with your parents, as difficult or as downright impossible as it seems to be.

But it may not be all that hard. First, why not take some time to look at your plans and your parents again? Are your plans really all that difficult to talk about, or do they just appear to be at first glance? Have you really got your parents in focus? Are they genuinely unreasonable? Actually possessive? Actually bad-tempered? Or are these the names you've given to what is really a deep and loving—though perhaps badly expressed—concern for your welfare?

Honest answers to questions such as these may help you to see your plans and your parents in a new light and make the idea of a talk not so impossible after all.

Even if they don't, there's still a chance. If you still feel that your parents won't listen or that your plans will outrage them, can you get some help? Suppose that your father is the difficult one. Can you appeal to your mother, win her support, and then together approach your father? Or is there a relative willing to speak on your behalf and pave the way for you? Or a trusted and respected friend of the family? Or a priest or minister? Or one of your teachers whom your parents admire?

Perhaps one or a combination of these suggestions will work. Perhaps they'll trigger other, better ideas. But, whatever the case, try to talk with your people. Try the "Five Steps to Independence," being gentle and kind while at the same time being frank and quietly determined in your resolve to leave. Don't push the issue if you see that you're getting nowhere at first. Withdraw for a while—even a few days—and give your parents time to get used to all that you've told them. Since your plans are on the difficult side, your people may need an extra bit of time to get used to them.

Do all this and you'll know that you've done your utmost to make your departure a graceful one. You'll have done your part to reduce hurt and anger. You'll have done your best to keep the lines of communication open, so that, should things change in the future, you'll all be able to get back together again with the least emotional wear and tear. And you'll always be able to look at yourself in the mirror and know that, as a young adult, you met your problem as honestly and as openly as you knew how.

Are you shaking your head along about now? Are you thinking, "All this is okay for somebody else. But not for me. My problem's just too tough."

But is it?

With a little thought, you can find something good to say about practically any plan, even the ones that parents find most difficult to accept. The idea here is not necessarily to win your parents' approval (though they may surprise you). Rather, what you're after is the next best thing —an understanding of and a sympathy for your views, aims, and motives. That understanding and sympathy may make it easier for your people to let you go, even while not fully approving of what you're going to be doing.

But what can you say, exactly? To get some ideas, let's look at three of today's most common and difficult problem areas. Let's say that you (1) intend to go to a commune or practice a religion strange to the family, (2) want to live with a loved one without marriage, or (3) plan to leave a divorced or widowed parent.

Communes and Gurus

After all that's been said and written in recent years, a parent really can't be blamed for going to pieces when you announce that you're settling in a commune or taking up a religion he thinks of as "oddball." Both have poor public images.

Take the commune by itself. You know what's said of it: Its housing is primitive at best, squalid at worst. In the country, it's to be found in a broken-down farmhouse or a collection of tents or tepees, with battered VW buses scattered all around. In the city, there it is in some ramshackle building or rat-infested tenement, love posters on the wall, and mattresses and sleeping bags on the floor. Its people have no money, wear funny clothes, eat nuts and berries, smoke marijuana, never take a bath, never marry, and do nothing but play guitars, make up Bob Dylan songs, and swap sleeping partners on whim.

The image of religious activity is even more disturbing. Again, you know what's been said and written. Those young people singing hymns in a field or passing out pamphlets on a street corner are "Jesus freaks." That young practitioner of Zen, seated cross-legged in the park with his eyes closed in meditation, is an object of amusement to the busy, practical world passing by. Those young people with the shaven heads and long robes of the Hare Krishna do not even deserve amused glances; due them are the stares reserved for the outcast. The young people of the Moon sect are brainwashed, with all contact with the family lost.

Against a backdrop of such unhappy images, you bet it's difficult to speak up on behalf of your commune or your religious belief. It's more than difficult in the light of one fact: While much of the reputation is undeserved, there is much of it that *is* deserved. The news reports of the unsanitary conditions and the diseases such as hepatitis that have been found in many communes are not lies. The sober news coverage of Moon's Unification Church leaves no doubt that the leaders do exert too much control over their followers, do make them prisoners—albeit willing prisoners—and do cut off their contacts with the family and the outside world.

Poor as they are, though, the public images give you a key as to what can be said to your parents. What's needed is to look at your commune or your beliefs and pick out for mention those healthy facets in them that don't fit the public image. As the old song says, you need to "accentuate the positive."

For instance, there's no doubt that you'll be an "outsider" if you shave your head and wear the Krishna robe. The same does not apply, however, if you've chosen a belief such as Zen Buddhism. But your parents may think it does. So why not tell them the truth of the matter—that you'll be able to practice your faith while holding a job, going to school, or doing any number of other ordinary daily things. Your beliefs, your meditations, your dietary habits may make you extraordinary in some eyes and amusing in others, but they won't make you an outcast. And, in time, they may win you the admiration of many a "straight."

As for communes, I've seen some that are downright filthy, with the members living in ways that would insult the most primitive of tribes. But I've also seen some that are models for healthy living.

I especially remember one about sixty miles north of San Francisco. It stands on three acres of ground that holds vegetable gardens, an orchard, a large old house, and a workshop. The house has a casual, untidy look to it because fifteen to twenty young people live there. But it's clean, as are the young people. They live an active life, turning out furniture and doing repairs in their workshop, tending their grounds, and attending school or going to outside jobs. Some are married, some are living together, but there appears to be nothing promiscuous in their behavior. The partners in each couple are committed to each other. Everyone is dedicated to a set of principles and beliefs that are studied and discussed daily. The whole place seems as much a school as a commune.

What if your commune is like this one—or at least something like it? Then tell your parents what life is like there. Or show them pictures of the place. Or, better yet, take them out and let them see it for themselves. Let them meet and get to know the young people there. Parents are like everyone else; they fear the unknown. A familiarity with your surroundings and your friends may be all that is needed to put many worries to rest.

But are you afraid that your friends will make fun of you if you arrive with your parents? Ask them and find out. You may learn that parental visits aren't all that unusual. If your friends do show scorn, then perhaps you should take a second look at them. In common with most young people today, they'll probably profess a belief in love and kindness for all. Aren't they being hypocritical if they can't extend that love and kindness to two people whose worry is based on love for you?

Most young people, when speaking of an alternative way of life, talk of what they hope it will do for them. This is fine. But, if you can do it with truth, try to go a step further. Tell your parents what your beliefs or your friends in the commune have *already* done for you. Have they changed your life in any way? Are you less selfish than before? Are you off the drugs that once caused so much heartbreak in the family? Is there now a direction to your life that wasn't there before? Is there a love and gentleness in your nature where there was once only anger and frustration? Is there happiness where there was only sadness?

Don't be afraid or embarrassed to talk about these things with your parents. Be just as open and revealing with them as with your closest friends. Better yet, because example is always more effective than words, let your parents *see* the changes that are taking place in you. Let your new modes of behavior speak for you and do their part in winning sympathy—and perhaps even support—for your cause.

Now what if you can find nothing positive to say about your plans?

Then it's time to have a talk not with your parents but with yourself. There's obviously something wrong at core with a life-style that can't be praised in some way. Perhaps, after all, it deserves that unhappy public image and needs to be closely questioned. The commune that seems so inviting—on cold second thought, is it really a carelessly maintained place whose unsanitary conditions will disgust you in a matter of days or weeks? Your friends there—are they really dedicated to a cooperative way of life or do just two or three handle all the work while the rest sit around thinking beautiful thoughts? The beliefs and practices of your religious group—are they really substantial or, on investigation, will they prove half-baked, spiritually empty?

As usual, this sort of penetrating examination may turn up some truths that you don't like or don't want to look at. But go ahead and look. And then try to act on them. They may save you from making a mistake that will be a problem to undo later.

One question may prove more significant than all the rest as you take this "second look" at the life you're choosing. All communes and religious groups are like families in at least one respect. They're organizations; to function, they must have their rules, their disciplines, their work assignments. If the restrictions at home have been bothering you, then you should assuredly ask yourself: Am I entering a life whose strictures and demands will soon prove just as suffocating as those at home—or even more so?

A last thought: Promise your parents that if life in the commune or with the religious group doesn't work out you won't hesitate to break free. This will not only ease their worries but will constitute a promise to yourself that will make it easier for you to act decisively should you eventually find that you've changed your mind or made a mistake. You won't lose precious time deciding what to do but will be able to move quickly to a new and, for you, more suitable life.

Living Together

The idea of living together without marriage, so popular among today's young men and women, has become a source of widespread debate among parents.

Some parents oppose the idea strongly, saying that marriage is a God-designed plan for living and that those who bypass it are damaging their moral fiber and destroying that age-old and most basic of social units, the family. Others feel that the young couples are selfish and immature, wanting the sexual intimacies of marriage while avoiding the commitments of marriage. The parents of the young woman involved often worry that she may be left with the burden of a child should the male get tired of it all and leave. As one mother acidly put it about her daughter's experience, "Everything was fine and dandy until there were diapers to wash. Then you should have seen how fast he headed for the hills. He may have done the same thing if they were married. But he also may have thought twice . . . may have had a greater sense of responsibility."

On the other hand, many parents see no harm in living together. In fact, some see certain advantages in it. They argue that if the young people decide to break up, there isn't the hassle of a divorce. Or they feel that a period of living together is beneficial if a marriage is planned; the partners get to know each other's strengths, weaknesses, and idiosyncracies on a day-to-day basis. With this experience behind them, they are better equipped to handle the burdens of married life.

My job here isn't to talk about who is right and who is wrong. The decision to live together belongs to you and your loved one. The only question of concern is: What can you do to break the news to your parents without causing an explosion that could go on exploding for months or years to come?

To get some answers, I turned to three young couples. Here, picked from long and informal conversations, are the main points they made.

Matt and Shelley lived together for eleven months before marrying two years ago. "I'd say, first things first," Matt advised. "Introduce your mate to your parents and let them get to know her. Or him. It sure helped in our case . . ."

Shelley: "Matt and I met when we were sophomores in college. We started living together in our junior year. My folks were appalled when they heard about it, especially my dad. I'm sure he thought Matt was just a letch after his little girl's body. But he changed his mind when he met Matt and saw how serious he was about his studies and a career in accounting. It was the same with my mother. She admitted to me that she thought Matt was the nicest boy I'd ever brought home."

Matt added that his parents reacted in much the same way to Shelley. Again, as was said about communes, it's a case of parents being human and fearing the unknown. Once the unknown becomes known, the fear usually starts to disappear.

"You might go even further," Les suggested. He and Paula have been married for six months. Starting when they were twenty, they lived together for over a year. "You might introduce both sets of parents to each other. Everybody sees that the kids come from good or matching backgrounds. Everybody likes everybody else. It can make things easier all around . . . And it could be that maybe one set of parents isn't so morally shocked or uptight as the other about the whole deal. Their attitude could help the other parents to soften their views."

Paula conceded that the idea might be a good one. But she worried a little. "I'd be sure of what I was doing before I tried that. You could end up with four people that don't like each other. Or they may all be uptight. Then you've got twice as much trouble. It's okay, I guess. But make certain of what you're doing . . ."

"Okay," Les said. "Then how about this one? It worked for us. Look, we weren't like Matt and Shelley. We didn't start living together and then have our families find out about it. We were each living at home when we made the decision. Each of us had to go through packing and leaving, and both our families knew we were moving in together. Man, it was pretty tacky."

"Was it ever!" This from Paula.

"That is, until we were settled in our own place. Then we had our parents over—one set at a time . . . That's when things started to change. I don't know what they expected, but I think they expected to find us living in a tent or something and eating off a packing crate. But, anyway, Paula's folks saw that I knew how to repair a kitchen faucet and paint a wall. And I know that my mother was relieved to see the dinner that Paula turned out . . . She finally got it into her head that I wasn't eating McDonald's hamburgers and TV dinners three times a day . . ."

Paula was nodding vigorously. "What Les is saying is that they began to see that we were living in the same way as a married couple. To them, I think we must have started to look like a family on our own."

Lloyd is twenty-one and Marian nineteen. They've lived together for about four months and intend to marry. Marian said, "Most of the young togethers we know are planning to be married. They're very committed to each other. I'd advise anyone to tell this to their parents. I think parents won't be half so shocked or worried if they know the kids are going to get married, and if they know they are committed to one another in all ways, just like good married couples are. It's the sex thing that's the big hang-up for most parents. They feel better if they know there's something more to the relationship than just shacking up and jumping into bed."

I had a question: "What if none of these steps work?"

Lloyd looked thoughtful for a moment. "I think they'll work—to one degree or another—if you've got understanding parents or if they can remember how it was between them when they were young. These things are certainly worth a try. In fact, anything is worth a try and is certainly better than doing nothing and letting everything fester—unless you've got the sort of parents who are happier pretending that nothing's going on when they know damn well there is. Then it's probably best to keep your mouth shut until you're ready to marry . . .

"If your people are way uptight and nothing works, then you've got no choice but to do what seems right for you. I'd always be kind to them, though . . . it won't be so hard for you all to get back together again if you have a breakup or after you're married."

Leaving the Single Parent

As the child of a single parent, you may feel that, more than anyone else, you're really in a bind when the time comes to talk of leaving. Were your parents together, they would at least have each other for company once you've gone. But your single parent will be left alone, deprived of your companionship and help around the house. Very quickly, there can be the guilty feeling that you're abandoning a loved one who needs and depends on you.

This feeling may be especially strong if you're a girl who is keeping house and cooking for a divorced or widowed father. Or if you're a son who believes—or has been told—that you're "the man around the house," the protector of a mother alone. Or if you're a boy or girl who is receiving a deceased parent's Social Security benefits. You know that the money is needed to maintain the household and that it's going to end when you depart.

Indeed, you *are* in a bind. You want your independence. But you feel guilty already and you realize it's going to get worse when you leave. And so you hesitate to talk with your parent. Yet you know that you must talk soon, must make your bid for freedom. Otherwise, you may end up trapped in the house for years to come, perhaps for the lifetime of the parent.

There's no need to say here that you should break the news of your intentions with gentleness and love. The very same sensitivity that makes you now worry about your parent's future welfare will take care of the manner in which you speak. Your problem, rather, is to overcome the sense of guilt that can keep you from talking in the first place. It can be overcome—in great part or in total—if you will keep firmly in mind a basic truth about independence.

Many people do remain at home with a single parent (or with both parents) well into adulthood. Some spend their entire lives with their parents. There's not a thing wrong with this, so long as it is natural to the people involved and so long as they are happy with the arrangement—and many are.

But, for the vast majority of people, the want for independence in adulthood is a *normal* and *healthy* impulse. Were it not, there wouldn't be the frustrations we see when a young adult remains in the nest too long. And the moving out to independence is a normal and healthy act. Further, independence isn't only normal and healthy for the young adult. It's quite as much so for the parents, en- abling them—singly or as a couple—to enter the next phase in their lives. They've borne the responsibilities of parent- hood for many years and at last have raised their children. It's time for new adventures, new pleasures.

If you have the courage to suppress your emotions and face this truth about independence, it should quiet any guilt long enough for you to speak with your parent. A guilt cannot long endure in the face of the recognition that what you want to do is the normal, healthy, and— hence—right thing to do.

Then, to your surprise, you may find that your parent shares the same understanding. The parent may want to see you live through the same enjoyments and challenges that he or she lived through, years earlier. Or the parent may know that, only with independence, can you fully de- velop. Or may know that the two of you can only grow if you make individual lives for yourselves.

Or you may be surprised, even shocked, to find that your parent is relieved to see you go, but has never spoken up for fear of making you feel unwanted. Many single par- ents want to try a new life-style, change careers, make new friends, travel, or enjoy a new love life, but feel that they can't rightfully do so until they're alone and no longer responsible to their children. So don't be hurt if you see relief. Wanting his or her independence, your parent is being just as normal as you are in wanting yours.

On the other hand, don't give up in defeat if you see

that your parent is going to be lost without you. If the parent has any personal strength at all, that sense of loss will be temporary, lasting only until he or she finds new interests and starts to build a new life. Most parents have this personal strength.

Should your parent refuse to call on that strength, however, you may still be able to leave with a clear conscience. Look closely to see if you're up against the parental version of what used to be called "the clinging vine wife"— that someone who enjoys being weak and being catered to. If so, remember there is no law of love that says you must sacrifice your happiness, individuality, and dreams for anyone who, though perfectly capable of doing so, refuses to stand up and take hold of life.

But if help seems needed—or even if it isn't—why not lend your parent a hand in finding that new life? This can be not only an affectionate service to the parent but also one to yourself. Once that new life is launched, your conscience can indeed be clear. So why not point out those local groups where new social contacts can be made? Why not discuss your parent's interests—political, social, artistic —to see where they can be put to use? If you've been cooking for your father, why not show him how to handle himself in the kitchen or encourage him to take a cooking class at the local evening school? And if your mother knows nothing but housework, why not encourage her to train for a skill that has a place on the job market?

You can do one special job if you are receiving Social Security death benefits that will end when you leave.

These monies can be especially important to a widow, and their loss can be critical. But, in many areas, there are public funds and programs available to help. You'd be wise to ask your local family agency for information on any type of aid for which your mother may be qualified until her financial position improves.

All these tasks may take time and effort. And it may take time and effort for your parent to grow accustomed to living without you, and time and effort for you to get completely over the feeling that you're abandoning someone who needs you. But they are more than worth the goal—a full, valuable, and exciting life for each of you.

If You Must Take Off

Though these ideas have all been centered on just three of today's problem areas, I hope they will be of help to you. Hopefully, in them you will glimpse ways in which you can successfully approach your parents with your own problem plan and avoid the anger and hurt that come with packing up and just taking off.

But now let's look at the bleakest side of the picture.

Let's say that you try to talk with your parents and that no one listens. You run up against anything from hostile silence to tears, a fainting spell, or a drinking bout. There's no mistake about it now. You're right back where you were at the start of this chapter. If you're to have your independence, you're left with no option but to take off.

Okay. Then leave you must.

But try to leave in a certain way. Try to leave with love.

Try to leave in such a way that the lines of communication remain open for a future reconciliation when everyone has had a change of mind or heart.

At first glance, this may look pretty impossible. Perhaps even silly. But it might not prove so impossible if you do as Joan did. Today, she's a legal secretary, living alone but on the best of terms with her family. She took off a month after her eighteenth birthday.

Her situation was especially difficult because of a parental possessiveness that turned to blind anger and frustration when she insisted on her freedom. When your bags are packed, you may be able to win a last-minute reconciliation as you say goodbye, but things were so bad for Joan that she had to march out without a word. Still, she just didn't disappear. She left a note. In it, she explained again why she wanted to try life on her own, expressed her regret that her parents objected, and established a time when she would telephone with news of how she was doing. She set the time for the call as soon after the departure as possible.

Then she made sure that she got on the phone at *exactly* that time, knowing that she'd worsen matters by worrying her parents that something had gone wrong if she was late. She told them that she was fine. She filled them in on the details of a job she had landed in a cafeteria, a job that would tide her over while she attended a secretarial school. She patiently answered their questions and did her best to soothe their fears and angers.

She had rented a small apartment in another part of town and she went so far as to invite her parents over to see how well she was doing. You may want to do the same thing or, if you see that tempers are still running high, you may want to keep your address to yourself for a while longer. If you don't wish to risk a visit just yet—or if you're too distant for one—then set a time for your next phone call. And, even if there's a lot of "you've-made-us-feel-terrible" talk at the other end of the line, try not to let your pride or impatience stop you from saying that you plan to call again. Just work to keep the lines of communication open. With the lines open, wounded feelings will have the best chance to heal themselves and come to want a reconciliation.

Joan thinks that a date for a get-together or a next call is the most important point of all. It can erase much hurt or bitterness by proving that you want to stay in touch and that you're not disappearing for good, never to be seen again. And, between now and the time of the date, your parents will have the chance to start getting used to the fact that you can survive alone and that life isn't ending for them just because you've left.

Time may be all that is needed. A new set of healthy relationships could be in the making.

Now that we have talked about the problems of taking off if you're of a legal age to do so, let's turn to the opposite side of the coin—to your problems if you're underage and a runaway.

4

About Running Away

No one knows exactly how many children and young people run away from home in the United States each year. But such organizations as the FBI estimate that the number ranges from at least 600,000 to a tops of two million. In age, the runaways extend from seventeen all the way down to six.

Studies show that most runaways stay out for three days to two weeks, often living with friends. Many, if not most, return home on their own or ask their parents to come and pick them up. The younger ones, of course, are usually the first to return; the absences can stretch out for lengthy periods when older runaways have enough money to get by. More girls than boys are running away today.

There seem to be about as many reasons for running away as there are runaways. The reasons stretch from those that appear trivial—though the kids involved don't see them that way—to some that are downright tragic.

On the one hand, some young people take off because

they aren't allowed to stay out late at night. Some because they don't like household chores, aren't allowed to drive the family car, or are made to study for a certain time each night. Some because their parents don't seem to like their friends; one sixteen-year-old boy told me that his folks didn't say a thing, but that "they were always looking at us like they were smelling something bad because we had long hair and jeans." Some because they can't stand the idea of final tests or school itself. The two most popular months for running away are May and September.

On the other hand, some young people run away because life at home has become so bad or so hopeless that they can't tolerate it any longer. Some can't stand being continually abused by their parents—not just spanked or slapped now and again but actually beaten up. Some can't go on living with drunken parents or with parents who are continually fighting. And a great many can't go on living in an atmosphere where there is no communication—no real understanding and sympathy—between parent and child.

Many social workers say that a lack of family communication is one of the most common problems faced by the young person in today's high-gear society. They feel that many children who run away because of it are not really trying to escape their homes but are trying to attract their parents' attention. It's felt that they're really saying, "Hey, look at me. I need help."

Some workers believe that, no matter the reason for taking off, most runaways are not actually trying to escape from a home environment. Rather, they seem to be looking for a new kind of home, a new kind of family life. Some would like to be placed in a foster home. Some would like to return to their own homes, but want things there to be different than they were. One way or the other, they want to be a part of a family that is close and together.

Two young people were interviewed on this point sometime ago at a center for runaways in Washington, D.C. Their remarks were printed in a 1975 issue of the magazine, *U.S. News and World Report*. The boy was fourteen and the girl fifteen.

The boy said that there was "absolutely no way" that he'd go back to his parents. "I'm happier without them. I want a family, a foster family, not a master-slave thing of no trust like I had." He explained that, whenever he had run away before, his parents had said that he could come back under certain conditions—"always intolerable to me . . . cut my hair, stop wearing ragged clothes, keep my door open even when I'm dressing . . . Hassle on top of hassle . . . There isn't any conversation, only orders."

The girl said that she, too, preferred a foster home and then went on to describe what she wanted it to be like. "I want to go to a real home with parents who are understanding and I don't want much fighting between them—especially in front of me. Parents just don't know what fighting in front of their kids does to the kid. My father used to try to choke me to death, and I've seen him do it to my mom. He never talks; he always yells. If he left, I'd go back to my mother. Otherwise, I want a foster home."

Over the years, I've talked with a number of young people who have run away, some several times. Almost without exception, they've said that running away is a hard route to take, even when conditions at home seem impossible. It's full of problems.

What Happens When You Run?

To begin, the law holds that parents have the right to raise their children as they see fit so long as they avoid neglect or serious physical abuse. If you run away, they have the right to come after you and bring you back. As for your own rights as a runaway, there is this famous statement made some years ago by a federal judge:

"An adolescent has the right to run away as far and as fast as his feet will carry him—until his parents catch up with him."

Your parents may use the police to help find you. They may also engage a private investigator if they can afford the cost. When using the police, they usually must wait forty-eight hours before reporting your disappearance. The waiting period is intended to give you some time to change your mind and return on your own. If you fail to appear, your people then file a missing person's report and the police issue a missing person's bulletin.

The bulletin contains your physical description and lists the clothes you were wearing when you took off. If you have any distinguishing marks—scars, moles, or a limp— they'll be mentioned. Any general information that the police think helpful may be included. Perhaps you like cars and have always tinkered around the local garage.

Information such as this will give the police in a distant city a hint as to where you may be found. Your picture may be attached to the bulletin.

Armed with the bulletin, the police may sight you at any moment. Even without it, they may stop you if they suspect you to be a runaway or a troublemaker. Perhaps you're loitering in the wrong part of town after dark or in any part of town after curfew. Perhaps you're slouched at a street corner. Perhaps you're sitting on a park bench, looking hungry and lost.

Once stopped, you can be taken in for any number of reasons. If the police have the missing person's bulletin, that's enough by itself. Without the bulletin, it's also enough if your I.D. shows you to be underage and you then can't prove that you're out with permission. The same applies if the police suspect your I.D. is a fake, if you qualify as a vagrant (no known address and/or no visible means of support), or if you're found to be living in unsafe and filthy conditions. If nothing else will work, they can fall back on the old tactic of holding you for questioning.

As soon as you're in custody, an attempt is made to get in touch with your parents. With the bulletin, the police can call the authorities in your hometown. Without the bulletin, your I.D. provides the needed lead. Some runaways with false I.D.s have tried to stall the police by giving false family names. Others have kept changing the names in an effort to confuse and delay matters. But, as one runaway told me, "It's a waste of time. Sooner or later, they're going to find out who you are—either from you because you finally get tired of playing games or from somebody or some place else."

Some runaways have heard about extradition (the process, sometimes difficult and time-consuming, of returning a wanted person to his home state from the state where he is now living) and think they'll be pretty safe if they can get across their state line. This isn't true. Most of the states now operate under what is called the Interstate Compact on Juveniles. It enables them to return runaways to their home state easily and quickly. Further, your parents can go to a court in your home state and file a petition for your return. The petition is sent to a court in the state where you're now living—and back home you go.

There is one way in which you can be prevented from being sent back to your home state quickly. Suppose that you've committed a crime in the state where you're now living. The state can hold you until you've been tried and served your sentence or until the charges against you are dropped. Then you're on your way home.

But do you have any rights at all? Yes—but just a few. For instance, let's say that you've fled from Pennsylvania to Ohio and your parents have filed a petition for your return. The judge in Ohio should tell you what's going on. He may also appoint a lawyer or a guardian to act on your behalf, and he may delay sending you back until he's had the chance to check the legality of your parents' petition. Or you may ask to have a lawyer represent you. He may be able to have you set free by showing that your rights as a citizen were violated by the manner in which you were taken into custody or by the length of time you were kept there. He may also be able to take steps to delay or prevent your return to Pennsylvania.

But, in either case, it's usually a losing battle. A judge faced with a petition or an attorney will most likely end up by turning you over to the Pennsylvania authorities. His reasoning will be simple: Since the Pennsylvania authorities are closer to your home, they'll be in the best position to work with you and your parents in squaring things.

Altogether, running away is a bummer for any young person. But what else can you do if life at home is impossible?

Solving Your Problem

For a start, you might do what a number of other young people have done. You might take a close look at your home and see what's really bothering you about it. With luck, the problem could turn out to be a small one—so small, in fact, that you may wonder what all the fuss has been about. But so what? Life's big problems are very often no more than a collection of small ones that get out of hand. The important thing is, you've identified the trouble. Now you can do something about it.

Just what you can do will depend on your exact problem. But you may be able to pick up a clue from some actual cases. They may fit—or come close to fitting—your situation.

First, there's fifteen-year-old Janet. Her gripe boiled down to the demand that she be home from dates by 10 o'clock. A lot of heartbreak was avoided when she sat down and, as calmly as she could, told her parents how she felt. A compromise was made—11 o'clock until she was sixteen, then midnight for a year, and finally 1 A.M. when she was seventeen. All restrictions were to be dropped when she reached the age of majority on her eighteenth birthday. It wasn't exactly the arrangement she wanted at the moment, but as she said, "It was one I could live with. At least, I knew things were going to get better as time went on."

Then there's Ben, sixteen years old and certain that his parents were watching his every move. In a burst of frustration one evening, he made his suspicions known. His father put an end to the problem simply by giving him a front door key of his own.

These are just two simple solutions to simple problems that, if left to fester, could have gotten completely out of control. Some solution just as simple may work in your case. Since you can't win a thing by running away, a talk with your folks is certainly worth a try. And you may be surprised at how much they'll give when you show your willingness to give a little yourself.

And if they won't give? Suppose you've got a real problem—an alcoholic parent, a cruel parent, an emotionally crippled parent, or a parent who can't stand the sight of you but still won't let you go? The solutions here are a lot tougher. But they can still be found.

Can you, for instance, do what Dave had to do when he was seventeen? The son of people who drank too much and fought too much, he had to make his decision to stay or leave on the basis of his aims in life. He wanted to attend college to study civil engineering, but he knew that, if he split, his chances for a state scholarship would likely go straight down the drain. He forced himself to sit where he was, gritting his teeth throughout his senior year at high school. Then, scholarship in hand, he made a graceful exit and headed for the distant state university.

But what if your situation has gotten past the teeth-gritting stage and you can't hang on as Dave did? Can you then, as Harry did when he was seventeen, land a summertime job in the mountains? The three months away from home eased the tension just enough for him to finish high school before enlisting in the Air Force. Or, as sixteen-year-old Mary did, arange to live with relatives for a time? Or with close friends of the family?

Among the most difficult problems of all is child abuse. Most often, its victims are younger children, but it has also made life miserable for many teenagers, especially those too small or timid to defend themselves. If it's a problem for you, there's nothing in the law that says you must stay quietly at home and take it. But you needn't run away either.

There's another solution.

All groups that work with the young—from the police to welfare agencies—recommend that you bring the problem to them and let them take care of it. Naturally, they don't want you running in because of a smack on the rear now and again, but they do want to help if you're being severely mistreated. The same goes if you're too big to be belted around but have a younger brother or sister who is being beaten.

As was said earlier, though your parents have the right to raise you as they see fit, they have no right to endanger your health and safety. Along with child neglect (which, likewise, should be reported if it's a problem), abuse is a criminal offense. With your report in hand, the authorities can take a number of steps to end it—all the way from warning the parents to removing the child from the home. The exact steps taken in an individual case depend on the seriousness of the situation.

Many children are afraid to report instances of abuse. Some fear parental reprisals. Others, despite all they've suffered, remain loyal to the family and fear that their parents will be publicly embarrassed or arrested. Still others fear that they themselves will be humiliated if word of their mistreatment gets out.

The juvenile authorities can help you avoid reprisals. If you're afraid of embarrassment to the family or yourself, you might take the advice that fifteen-year-old Janet took. It came from a police officer as he was speaking about the abuse problem to her social studies class. He said that it's best for an abused child not to go to the police but to the county probation office, which handles juvenile matters and is usually located in the county courthouse or civic center.

The police are perfectly capable of handling the matter, he explained, but they must write a report on it, just as they do on all cases. The report is a record that can easily reach the public. It may lead to the parents' arrest after an investigation, or word of it may find its way into the newspapers. But the probation office is usually able to handle the matter confidentially at the "family level," perhaps straightening things out by talking to the parents and warning them of the penalties that lie ahead if the abuse continues. Unless the matter is so serious that it must result in criminal charges, there need to be no public word to embarrass the child or the family.

If you don't wish to go to the probation office, you can try other avenues. There are the police, of course, even though they must write a report. There is the local welfare agency. In many towns, there are centers and "halfway houses" for runaways. It doesn't matter that you haven't run away yet—they'll be willing to help and advise you. Or you might try your family priest or minister. He may be able to talk with your parents or go to the authorities on your behalf.

If You Must Run

I hope that all I've written so far will help you to solve your problem without running away. The odds are all on your side that your problem—whether it be large or small—can be solved with some talk that leads to a new understanding and sympathy between you and your parents.

But you may be shaking your head. You may still feel that your problem is too big and has no solution. You may feel that you *must* run away.

If so, then at least try to keep a few points in mind when you leave. These points are not meant to encourage you to run away but to protect yourself in a bad time that can become worse with the slightest mistake or misstep on your part. I learned them while talking with a number of runaways and juvenile authorities.

Don't Break the Law

By itself, running away is not a criminal offense. Like staying out after curfew, it's known as a "status offense," and the whole aim of the law is not to punish you but to get you to safety and straighten out the trouble at home. As a runaway, though, you can easily get yourself into the sort of trouble that is classed as a crime.

You know you're in for trouble if you shoplift, break into a house for food or money, or hot-wire a car for a quick trip to the next town. But do you also know that you're in for trouble if you try to hide behind a false I.D.? You can be charged with "criminal impersonation," a misdemeanor that's punishable by up to a year in jail. And, of course, if you're using a stolen I.D., you're open for theft charges.

Should a policeman stop you, don't give him a bad time, even though you know he's going to end up taking you in as a runaway. Show him your identification and answer his questions. Don't argue with him, don't take a swing at him, or attempt to flee. Any of these actions may result in your being charged with "resisting arrest" or "resisting an officer." They're criminal charges.

As a runaway, you can get your friends into trouble. If you stay with someone who has reached the age of majority, he can be taken in for "contributing to the delinquency of a minor." If you're a girl, and have sexual relations with him, he is liable for a charge of statutory rape.

Don't Be Too Proud to Go Home

Should you change your mind a few hours or a few days after leaving, don't let your pride keep you from going home immediately. Every minute that you're away increases the possibility of getting into trouble. It may be difficult to go home in defeat, but life is going to be twice as rough if you run out of money, fall ill, or meet the wrong kind of people.

If you're a long way from home when you decide you've had enough, give your folks a telephone call (collect, if you're broke) and let them know you're returning. The call can accomplish quite a lot. It can relieve everyone, yourself included. It can give your parents time to calm down while you're returning and make your arrival a much less emotional one. It can enable them to call off the police search for you. And, of course, they'll be able to wire you money if it's needed, or come to pick you up.

Don't Be Afraid to Seek Help

Suppose that you can't bring yourself to go home. But you're broke, hungry, sick, or just fed up with being on the run. Then don't hesitate to go to the authorities and ask for assistance. In practically every city and town there are agencies that are in business to help runaways. They can provide—or show you where to obtain—shelter, food, clothing, medical attention, and legal advice.

There's little or no reason to be afraid of the authorities if you ask for help. Remember, running away is not a crime in itself. Even if you have done something wrong along the line, you'll likely be met with sympathy because you've shown the good sense to come in. The odds are that the authorities will see you as someone who wants to straighten out things, and they'll do as much as they can to help.

Where, exactly, can you go for assistance? First, don't shy away from the police. Every police department has juvenile officers and some have officers who deal exclusively with runaways. All these officers understand the runaway's problems and can give expert help.

As already mentioned, many cities have centers and "halfway houses" for the runaway. They can do many things for you, from providing shelter and counsel to serving as a mediator between you and your parents. Often arrangements can be made for you to stay with a foster family while the authorities look into your case and see what can be done to settle your problem.

If you can't locate a center and are reluctant to go to the police, you might turn to the local health and welfare departments. Or to such national groups as the YMCA, the YWCA, and the Salvation Army. There, too, are such religious organizations as the Catholic Youth Organization. They're all experienced in dealing with people in trouble. Some may be able to feed and temporarily shelter you, and all should be able to assist you in getting to the exact authorities needed. All these organizations can be found in the telephone book.

Suppose that you haven't got the money for a phone call. Then there are two toll-free numbers available to you.

They're called "runaway hotlines" and we'll be talking about them in a moment.

No matter how much you may need assistance, don't accept it from some "nice stranger" in the street. The chances are slim that he genuinely wants to help. More than likely, you're being hit by a pimp who plans to put you to work.

Broke and lonely, runaway girls are prime targets for prostitution. In New York and other cities, pimps are known to hire scouts to locate runaway prospects for them. You're especially vulnerable to an approach if you're sighted loitering on a street corner or sitting disconsolately on a park bench. You may even be approached the moment you arrive in a new city; some pimps and scouts think that bus and train depots are the best grounds of all for finding new talent or—to use their slang—new "packages" or "flat-backers."

The approach is always soft. The man tells you you're beautiful. He likes you, feels sorry for you, wants to be your friend. There are promises of a hot meal, a nice place to stay, and some pretty clothes tomorrow. Paid sex is never mentioned at this point. But don't fall for any of it. In a day or so, you'll meet the other girls in his "stable" and be told to get to work.

And don't think that you can go along with him for an hour or so, get a hot meal out of him, and then take off. The man is street-wise and he's seen that stunt before. Once he's got you, it's hard to get away and you'll be punished for trying. Girls who have attempted to escape or refused to work have been beaten, raped, burned with red-hot metal coat hangers, and made to perform degrading sex acts in front of the man's fellow pimps. In one well-known New York court case, five men and eight women were tried for raping and torturing four runaway girls who balked at joining a prostitution ring.

If you're a boy, you may think yourself safe from this sort of thing. Don't bet on it. It's a well-known fact that many young male runaways have been talked or forced into becoming prostitutes for homosexuals. In New York and elsewhere, male prostitutes are known as "chicken hawks."

Know the Hotline Numbers

Should you still have no idea of where to go for help, you need do no more than hunt up the nearest telephone booth. You can then dial either of two toll-free "runaway hotline" numbers.

The numbers will put you in touch with message centers at Chicago, Illinois, or Houston, Texas. Both centers were established several years ago because of the growing number of runaways in the 1970s. Both centers operate with public funds.

Wherever you may be, the Chicago center can help to arrange medical, legal, and shelter care for you. It will also deliver any messages that you may want sent to your family.

The Houston center's main job is to relay messages home, though it can also offer other assistance. Either center will take return messages from your parents and hold them until you call back. Even if you haven't relayed a message home, it's a good idea to call now and again to see if your parents are using the centers to get messages through to you. Both centers are also happy just to talk with you about your problem if that's all you want to do.

When you call, no pressure is exerted to have you return home. Your call isn't traced and the line isn't tapped. The single aim of both centers is simply to help you.

You can reach the Chicago center from outside Illinois by dialing 800-621-4000. The number for calls from inside Illinois is 800-972-6004.

When calling the Houston center from outside Texas, dial 1-800-231-6946. From inside Texas, call 1-800-392-3352.

Take Advantage of the New Thinking

This final point is perhaps the most important one of all. It comes into play once you've returned home.

More and more, today's juvenile authorities are recognizing the fact that it does little good just to return the runaway to his home. They understand that many young people run off because of some deep-seated problem in the family's life. The best thing that can be done is to help the family find that problem and solve it.

And so, when handling your case, the authorities may recommend that you and your parents get together for family counseling. The counseling, which may last for several months, is usually conducted by a local family agency, a clergyman, a psychiatrist, or a psychologist.

Counseling is something that seems to work for almost everyone. It's proving successful all across the country. If it's recommended for you and your parents, try to take full advantage of it. Cooperate to the best of your ability and hope that your parents will cooperate just as much. By your attitude and your interest, encourage them to do so.

There's an excellent chance that it will lead to the end of the problem that has caused you all so much trouble over the years.

5

Dollars and Cents

Now let's say that, instead of taking off or running away, you're planning to talk with your parents. You're getting ready to do so by settling down to work on that most important of the "Five Steps to Independence"—a plan for the future.

Unless you own stock in a few John Denver recordings, a number of pointed questions are sure to crop up almost immediately. They're all on one subject—money—and they'll probably come out like this:

Am I in a practical position to leave?

Have I enough money to get settled in a new place?

How much will I need to live from one end of the month to the other?

There's no need to say that money is important if you're going to be living by yourself. But you may be tempted to duck the questions if you're planning, say, to settle in with a friend or join a commune. Who needs cash for that sort of thing?

The answer: everyone. Whether with a friend or in a commune, you'll be expected to pull your own weight sooner or later. A friend may be willing to pay all the bills while you get your bearings, but there's sure to be the day when you hear the words, "Hey, I can't take the whole bite anymore. When are *you* going to do something?" In a rural commune, you'll not only be asked to lend a hand turning the ground, cooking, and developing the settlement, but you may also be called on to help meet the costs of clothing, doctors' bills, or food should the crops fail.

Also, you may soon decide that life with a roommate or in a commune just isn't for you and that you want to leave. Oscar Madison and Felix Unger may get along fine through comic thick and thin in "The Odd Couple." But that's television. This is life, and the best of friends—not to mention young couples who are married or living together—have been known to split up after two opposite personalities have shared the same space for a time. If you're a Felix, an Oscar roommate can be the same as a father whose ideas of life are limited to the next baseball game and his next can of beer. If you're an Oscar, a Felix can quickly become a mother who is always telling you to pick up after yourself.

And we've already talked about the problem of commune life. Remember, whether they be rural or urban, communes are structured like families, complete with their own rules, philosophies, and work assignments. You know the only choice you've got if the restrictions and the pressures to conform prove as stifling as those back home.

And so, no matter your sex, it's safest to have some

money set aside or coming in from a job. If you're by yourself, you won't have to go into debt or return home for anything but a visit. If you're living with others, you won't be a burden. And, if a change is called for, you'll be able to make it with some ease.

But money is hard to come by. Just how much will you need? The answer depends on your intentions. Are you going to live alone or with a friend? Or join a group? Have a car? Continue your education? Go to another city? Marry?

You can't help but take a look at your money situation as soon as you begin to work on your plan. You may find yourself asking more questions about money than about anything else in the plan. Perhaps you'll want to start with these and use them to open the way to others:

1. Can I really handle just yet all the financial responsibilities that come with independence—and the social and legal obligations that go with them? Do I, for instance, know the minimum amount of car insurance that the laws of my state require I carry? How much liability coverage should I have for the best protection of my passengers? What are the costs?

2. Do I really have enough money on hand to see my way through the heavy expenses always incurred in the first months of being on my own?

3. Will I really be able to continue my education or my training for a job if I'm on my own? I've set aside a year's tuition for a technical or a secretarial school. What's going to happen to it if I have to furnish an apartment? If the price of food jumps again? If I'm living with friends who insist that we throw a lot of expensive parties?

4. If I plan to rent with a friend, can I be reasonably sure

that he will hold up his end of things? Will his salary be enough to cover his share of the monthly bills? How responsible is he? What are the chances that I'll end up paying *all* the rent, *all* the utility and food bills?

The answers to these questions—and to others that will surely come to mind—will indicate the course you'll need to take. You may find that you're in excellent financial shape and can be on your way immediately. Or you may decide to remain at home a while longer while getting into a stronger position. Or you may find that you can make it by yourself or with a roommate if you budget tightly and give up certain luxuries.

To help you make these decisions, let's take a hard look at the monthly expenses that can be expected with independence. For the hardest look possible, let's say that you're planning to take the most expensive route there is.

You're planning to go it alone, with no one to share the costs with you.

The Monthly Bite

Some of your expenses will come to mind immediately— food, gas and electric bills, telephone, and rent for your apartment. These are among the most obvious ones, but they're just a few of the many that you'll be running into each month.

The easiest way to see what the whole bundle will be is to start with the three general categories into which all expenses can be divided. From there, we'll get down to the actual bills themselves. The three categories are:

1. Fixed expenses
2. Variable expenses
3. Special funds

Fixed expenses are those that remain the same every month, while variable expenses are those that, as their name suggests, vary with the month or crop up periodically. Special funds are those that are put aside for general savings, vacations, special purposes, and the like. Though called special funds here, you'll also hear people refer to them as "accumulating funds," "rainy day money," or even "the war chest."

The list below will give you an idea of the kinds of expenses that fall within each category:

FIXED EXPENSES

1. Rent or home payment
2. Insurance payments
3. Installment payments
4. Allowance for family members
5. Taxes
6. Church and charities

VARIABLE EXPENSES

1. Household expenses (food, etc.)
2. Utilities
3. Car (maintenance, repair, etc.)
4. Clothing
5. Medical and dental
6. Recreation and entertainment

SPECIAL FUNDS

1. General savings
2. Specific purchases

3. Christmas
4. Vacation
5. Investments

Once you're acquainted with the three categories, you can begin to take your first real look at what it's going to cost to live each month. To do this, draw up a chart that's based on the list above, but make room in it for specific bills that you're now paying, along with those that you can count on paying when you're on your own.

Here's an expanded chart that you can use as a guide. As you make out your own chart, don't bother to put down the money figures just yet. Wait until you've read the four points that follow the sample chart. Then you'll do a more complete job.

FIXED EXPENSES

1. Rent or home payment $_____

2. Insurance payments
   a. Life $_____
   b. Health   _____
   c. Dental   _____
   d. Car   _____
   e. Other   _____   _____

                   _____

3. Installment payments
   a. Car $_____
   b. Department stores _____   _____

                        _____   _____
   c. Other   _____   _____

                        _____   _____

4. Allowances $_____

5. Taxes   Federal $_____
              State $_____
              Local (property
              taxes, etc.) $_____

6. Church and charities   _____ $_____

        _____   _____

VARIABLE EXPENSES

1. Household expenses
    a. Food $_____
    b. Supplies _____

2. Utilities
    a. Heat $_____
    b. Electricity _____
    c. Water _____
    d. Garbage collection _____
    e. Telephone _____

3. Car
    a. Gas and oil $_____
    b. Maintenance _____
    c. Repair _____

4. Clothing $_____

5. Medical and dental $_____

6. Recreation and entertainment $_____

SPECIAL FUNDS

1. General savings $_____

2. Special purchases   _____ $_____

        _____   _____

3. Christmas		$_____
4. Vacation		$_____
5. Investments	_____	$_____
	_____	_____
	TOTAL	$_____

Now for those four points:

First, don't let the length of the chart discourage you. It's been made long not only to cover all possible present expenses but to give you a solid idea of the many kinds of expenses you will encounter throughout life. Some areas will not apply to you immediately, while others may never apply. For instance, you won't have to worry about a local property tax until you own a home, a building, or a piece of land. Put down figures only in those areas that apply to you, but fill them in as accurately and as completely as possible.

Second, perhaps you're now making several periodic payments—say, for a car insurance premium that falls due quarterly, or a tuition payment that must be made each semester. To learn what each represents in per-month money, divide the amount due annually by twelve. If you're saving up the payments a little at a time, you'll see how much you should set aside monthly to have enough on hand when each bill comes due.

Third, if you haven't much of an idea of utility costs, invest a little time in phone calls to the local utility companies to learn something of their charges, both initial and monthly. Of course, your monthly charges will depend on how much you use a given utility, but at least you'll get a beginning estimate.

You can also get some help here from friends already living independently. Or what about your parents? They're veteran bill-payers. Incidentally, something as simple as asking them about utility bills can put your parents on your side and make them a part of the solution to the problem of your departure.

Once you've collected the needed information, estimate the charges a little on the high side in your chart. You may save yourself a financial pinch later on.

The same attention should be given to food, clothing, and all other items whose costs are unfamiliar to you.

Finally, if you've just gotten your first job and have yet to receive a salary check, be prepared for a striking difference between your actual pay and your take-home pay. Avoid the mistake made by the inexperienced worker who added up his expenses and said, "Good. It's going to cost me $450 a month to live and I'm going to be earning $500. No problem." He now remembers, "Man, was I wrong. I wasn't taking home anywhere near $500."

The amount of your take-home pay will, of course, be determined by the number of deductions made from your salary. There are several that you can expect, chiefly those for taxation and Social Security (FICA). Others will depend on whether your company has a retirement system and whether you take advantage of such fringe benefits as health and life insurance coverage. Altogether, they can cut into a $500-a-month salary to the tune of $150 to $200 or more.

It's a sizable chunk—and especially so for someone who's counting pennies to make sure that the money doesn't run out ahead of the month.

What About a Car?

Some of the biggest figures on your chart can be those for your car. Considering its purchase price and the costs of gasoline, oil, repairs, and insurance, an automobile can end up being the single most expensive item in your life, eating up as much money a month as your apartment rent, if not more. And so, before doing anything more with the chart, let's talk a little about wheels.

Without really thinking about it, many young people feel that they'll need a car for work and pleasure when they're living on their own. But is this really true? Is an automobile always necessary?

Much of the answer depends on where you plan to live. Suppose that you're heading for a city like New York or Chicago. There, a car can be more of a hindrance than a help. Wherever you go, you'll likely be inching along in heavy traffic. There'll always be a parking problem when you go shopping, to work, or out on a date. If your apartment is in a central area, you probably won't have garage space and you'll have to leave your pride and joy out at the curb every night, collecting dust and inviting the attention of every vandal that wanders by—that is, if you can find an open stretch of curb. Or you'll have to garage it in some public facility and pay a fortune for the privilege of doing so.

All things considered, a car doesn't look too good in

cities such as these—and especially when you know that they've got pretty good mass transportation systems that can get you about more quickly and less expensively. And especially when you know that the central areas are confined enough to enable you to walk to many places, not only getting there just as swiftly but picking up some exercise in the bargain.

On the other hand, let's say that you're going to some place like Los Angeles. Now you're in a sprawling area that doesn't have adequate mass transit. It's put the emphasis on the car by building one of the best freeway systems in the country. If you rent an apartment near school or your job, you can manage without a car for a time. But you're going to want and need one sooner or later—probably sooner. Otherwise, as a friend of mine says, "It can take you so long to get to work by bus or streetcar that you can turn old and gray before punching in."

If you're planning to start life on your own in an unfamiliar place, it will be a good idea to talk to someone who now lives there. Or, if it isn't too far away, you might invest a little time and money in a visit. Find out how necessary a car is going to be. Then you can decide whether to start saving for a purchase or to come a few dollars ahead by selling the car you now own.

And, if you're planning to stay around your home area, why not take a new look at it? Even though you might be used to getting about in the family car, will you really need wheels of your own for work and a full social life?

Raised in the generation of the car, you know full well how much it costs to buy, either new or used. And you know what the bite for gasoline and repairs can be. But there is one expense that you may not be too familiar with because your parents have been handling it so far—insurance. It can really hit you hard.

For the protection of everyone on our crowded roads, all states have what is usually called a financial responsibility law. It demands that any driver in an accident be able to show proof that he can pay a certain minimum amount toward the injuries and property damages suffered by the other parties. In most states, the financial responsibility law must be obeyed by holding an insurance policy that meets the minimum amount. In a few states, you may carry insurance or post some other type of security—usually a bond—in the minimum amount.

The minimum amount needed to meet the financial responsibility law varies among the states. For instance, many states demand that their drivers be covered for $5,000 in property damages and up to $30,000 for all persons injured, with a limit of $15,000 per person. Other states require coverage for $5,000 in property damage, but go up only to $20,000 for all people injured, with a limit of $10,000 per person.

Costly though the insurance to meet these limits is, you must carry it in sufficient amount to satisfy the law. Otherwise, you're vulnerable for some stiff penalties should you be in an accident—plus having to live with a troubled conscience for failing to provide for those whom you've hurt or whose property you've damaged. Your driving license may be suspended. Your car may be impounded and the storage fees charged to you. Your license plates and your registration may be taken away. Then, if you're caught driving with a suspended license, you may be fined or jailed—or fined *and* jailed.

When you first talk to an insurance agent about covering your car, he'll likely say that you'll be pretty safe in taking out insurance just above the minimum amount required by your state. This is because you're just getting started in life and not yet earning too much. Most anyone involved in a traffic mishap of your making will know that you personally haven't the money to pay a fortune in damages and injuries. The other driver may want to ask for $50,000, but, realizing that he'll never be able to get that much, will be content to settle for just the amount covered by your insurance. As you grow older, though, you should increase the amount of your insurance.

The reasoning here is that you can expect to acquire more wealth as you go along. Perhaps, in ten to fifteen years time, you'll have a high-paying job or a business of your own, plus a home and various investments. Then, should the injured someone ask for $50,000 or more, he'll know that you have the money. If you have to pay him and if you've still got, say, just $15,000 in injury coverage, the insurance company will come up with that amount only and you'll be stuck for the remaining $35,000. By paying it, you may ruin yourself financially for years to come, if not for the rest of your life.

Unfortunately—and here's where your living expenses can really be hit—insurance rates are extraordinarily high for the young because statistics show that drivers in their teens and early twenties are the most accident-prone of all motorists. There's no way for us to figure exactly how high your own rates will be. Too many individual factors are involved. But they'll come out as soon as you sit down with an agent to fill out an application.

He'll want to know, for instance, how far you drive to and from work daily. He'll want to know whether you drive mostly in a crowded city, in a suburban area, or out in the country. And he'll ask about your driving record: how many traffic citations have you received and how many accidents have you had in, say, the past three to five years? All your answers are put together to fashion a statistical picture that tells the insurance company how great a risk you're going to be.

If your driving record is poor, you may be tempted to lie about it. But it's a waste of time—and a dangerous one. Each insurance application is checked with the state's Department of Motor Vehicles. If what you've said doesn't tally with the department's records, you'll be denied the insurance. If you tell the truth, you'll probably have to pay a still higher rate, but at least you'll have the chance of being insured in the first place.

Though we can't say here what your rates will be, you might get a beginning idea by asking your parents what they pay for their insurance. But don't stop there. Get ready to do some multiplying. A friend of mine who is an insurance agent says that it's not unusual for the young person to pay at least *three times* what the older adult is charged for the very same coverage. Ouch!

Now for a last point that may be of help: As a member of the car generation, you not only know the price tags on new and used cars, but also probably know what to look for or guard against in a car when the time comes for a purchase. But should you need some extra help, I suggest that you turn to the book, *Consumer Reports*. It is published annually in paperback, costs $3 as of this writing, and can be obtained in any bookstore.

In it, you'll find an excellent chapter that rates the engine, body, fuel, and repair performance of all new and used cars on the American market. The chapter also contains a series of excellent common-sense pointers on how to pick out a good and serviceable used car. It can save you from making some costly mistakes.

Me? On a Budget?

Now back to the chart. Once you've completed it and compared its total with your monthly income, you'll know pretty well where you stand financially. If you're lucky, you'll have more than enough to get by. But, if you're like most everyone else, you'll have to start making some adjustments—downward. Perhaps you'll have to set less aside for clothing. Perhaps hold off buying that stereo set. Perhaps settle for hamburger three nights a week.

If so, welcome to the club. You're on your way to living on a budget.

The idea of a budget turns many young people off. Some complain that it deprives them of freedom. Others are sure that it locks them to the Establishment treadmill and turns them into the money-conscious dullards that their parents' friends seem to be.

Could be. But the fact remains that the personal budget

is the best—perhaps the only—method for efficiently con-
trolling your money. Remember, the big thing you're
working for is an independence that's permanent. The
budget can enable you to handle what little money you do
have with a wisdom that will put the odds for permanence
all on your side.

There are no hard-and-fast rules as to the form your
budget should take. It may be simple. It may be complex.
It may show just your expenses. It may show your expenses, your income, your savings, even your growing retirement fund at work—in a nutshell, everything that lets
you see your financial standing at a glance. The form is
entirely up to you. All that it need be is one that you like
and that works successfully for you.

But, whatever that form turns out to be, there are three
common-sense rules that should be followed when keeping a budget.

1. Keep the budget in writing and maintain it carefully
from month to month. Don't just put it in your head and
trust it to memory. Unless the whole thing is on paper,
you'll find it too easy to make an unwise purchase simply
by forgetting some debt currently owed or some bill coming up sooner than you thought. How you keep the budget
is your choice—in a folder, a loose-leaf binder, a notebook,
or a bound record book. What counts is that it be in writing and carefully maintained.

2. The preparation of a budget is anything but an easy
task. Take your time with it and make it complete. As one
student has put it, "There's nothing more frustrating than
to finish your budget and then realize that you forgot

something. Me—I forgot the cost of my schoolbooks."

3. Your budget total, of course, should equal or fall below your income. Unless you're very lucky, you may need to make some pretty severe adjustments to bring it down to the desired level. Try your best, though, to make all the adjustments reasonable ones. If possible, avoid trimming any item to the point where you'll be unable to live with it.

If you think that any item has been cut too deeply, check your figures to see if any other areas can be reduced in its place. Your best guide here will be a realistic look at your personal tastes. If, for instance, you can't do without good food but care little for new clothes, then trim your clothing allotment while leaving a little more money assigned to food.

Living with Your Budget

Once your budget is drawn up, it will have to face the test of time. Will it really work? Will changes need to be made?

Certainly, as the months go by, you'll have to revise your figures to bring your estimates into final line. Because of the thought that went into the budget preparation, most, if not all, of the revisions should be minor ones, with some figures going up slightly and some going down.

Better than anything else, the revisions will make it clear why a budget should be kept in writing. You'll be able to put all the revisions down on paper and see your actual living costs at a glance. Avoided will be the confusion that comes of trying to keep a welter of figures straight in your head.

Again, you can keep your budget in any written form that you wish. But how best to develop a form that suits you? To help you answer that question, let's look at the experience of a young factory worker as he put together and then revised a budget. At the time, he and his wife were earning a monthly take-home pay of $670.

He began as you have. He listed all his expenses and called the list a "master budget." Then he bought a bound ledger and wrote the master budget on its first page, categorizing the items under "fixed," "variable," and "special" headings.

Next, he gave a page to each month as it came up on the calendar. In the left margin on a page he printed all the budget items as they appeared in the master budget. He divided the rest of the page into three columns, each with a special heading.

When he was done, the first lines for the month looked like this:

Fixed Expenses	Month's Allocation	Month's Spending	Ending Balance
Rent	140.00	140.00	0
Tuition	35.00	35.00	0
Life Insurance	20.00	0	20.00
Variable Expenses			
Food & Household	150.00	129.75	20.25

During the first months of living with the budget, he saw necessary adjustments. He noted them on the master budget and, when the next year rolled around, he wrote the revised master budget onto an appropriate page. Experience, too, had shown him that he needed additional columns on the monthly pages that followed.

Added were two new columns. The first was headed *Balance Brought Forward* and showed how much money was left over in any given area from the preceding month and so could be spent this month. The second, headed *Total Available*, gave the sum of the balance brought forward plus this current month's allocation.

The first lines of his budget for a month now looked like this, with all the rest of the entries listed in the same manner:

Fixed Expenses	Bal. Brought Forward	Month's Allocation	Total Available	Month's Spending	Ending Balance
Rent	0	140.00	140.00	140.00	0
Tuition	0	35.00	35.00	35.00	0
Life Ins.	20.00	20.00	40.00	40.00	0

He took one last step. At the bottom of each month's page, he listed his income, the interest on his savings accounts, the amounts withheld from the family paychecks for taxes, and the accumulating funds in his and his wife's retirement benefits at work. By doing so, he had on each page a complete picture of his financial situation.

As he put it, "It always let us know where we stood. And it always gave us a good feeling. We never failed to feel sort of rich when we looked at it."

All this is not to say that you must imitate the young man to have a successful budget. But, hopefully, it will help you on your way to developing a budget form of your own, one best-suited to your tastes and needs. Once it is developed, whether you're worker or student, married or single, living alone or with others, it will prove a major key to your independence—no, not just to your independence, but to your permanent independence.

6

Two More Keys

A budget is a major key to your independence, yes, but it's not the only one. A friend of mine who teaches economics in junior college has long told his students that it should be joined by two others.

Granted, he says, the budget keeps your money under an all-important control. But just as important is the second key, which is the use of a bank for safety, convenience, and that extra feeling of independence that comes with building some savings. The third is an understanding of how to handle and protect yourself when buying things on credit.

He tells his students, "If you can take care of all three, you'll do a good job of handling your money right from the start. You'll really cut down on the chances of running into trouble and maybe having to go home for a while."

So let's take a look at these two extra keys and see how they can be used.

You and Your Bank

Had you been born a few centuries ago, it's likely you would have kept your money at home, safeguarding it from thieves by stuffing it in a strong box and hiding it in a wall or under the floor.

Now, along with the vast majority of people, you deposit it in your account at the local bank. The bank holds the money in safety for your use and provides you with a continuing record of the funds you put in and take out. In effect, the bank serves as a community strong box, with your account being a personal "strong box" within it.

All banks offer a wide variety of accounts for their customers. Some, for instance, are intended for business funds, others for personal monies. But all accounts can be broken down into two basic types—checking and savings.

Your Checking Account

With a checking account, you're able to go about your daily business without carrying large sums of money on your person. You needn't hand over cash for the goods and services that you buy. Instead, you pay for each with a check, a piece of paper that orders your bank to pay to a person or an organization a certain amount of the money in your account.

Anyone who receives a check from you may turn it into cash in several ways. He may, for instance, take it to your bank for cashing. More often, he'll cash it at his bank or deposit it in his account there; the check is then forwarded to your bank to obtain the funds from your account. Or he may give it to a friend for cashing, after which it goes to the friend's bank and then finds its way to yours. Actually, the check may pass through several hands before even getting back to your bank.

Your check is every bit as good as cash so long as it is made out properly and so long as you have enough money in your account to cover it. If not made out properly, it won't be honored by the bank and probably won't be accepted for cashing in the first place by anyone with a knowledge of checking procedures. And if you don't have enough money on hand, the bank may return the check or may pay it and then charge you a penalty—$2 per check in many areas—for doing so.

To make the check out properly, you'll need to include five points in it. They're required by the laws that govern banking.

1. It must show a date. The check may be cashed only *on* or *after* that date. The bank is not allowed to honor the check prior to the date or if the date is omitted.
2. The check must include your signature. The signature should be exactly the same as the one specified in your account. If your account name is John K. Jameson, Jr., it should appear that way on the check and not as, say, Jack Jameson or John K. Jameson.
3. The name of the *drawee* or *payee*—the one to whom the check is made out—must also appear.
4. The amount of the check, of course, must be stipulated. It usually appears twice, once in numerals and once written or printed in full.
5. Finally, there must appear on the check a direct order to pay the money to the drawee. The law prohibits the bank

from handing out a customer's money without his instructions to do so. All checks issued by banks for use by their customers carry such necessary wording as *Pay to the order of, On order of,* or *Order of.*

Point 3 needs an extra bit of explanation. Though the space allotted for the drawee's name must be filled in, you need not always write in his actual name. Your check will be properly made out if, in place of his name, you use the word *Cash* or *Bearer* instead.

Suppose that, needing $50 from your account, you drop by the bank and write yourself a check for it. Rather than bothering to write your name twice, you can substitute the word *Cash* in the drawee space. Also, you may use *Cash* or *Bearer* if your check is to be cashed by someone who doesn't need or wish to have his name appear on it.

When you have a checking account, the bank at the end of each month sends you a *statement.* This is a printed record of your account. It usually covers a thirty- or thirty-one-day period and lists the amounts that you deposited in or removed from the account during that time. Accompanying it are the checks that the bank handled for you within the period. Once the bank has handled them, they're called *cancelled* checks. Every statement shows the following:

1. The number of your account.
2. The ending date of the period covered by the statement.
3. The number of deposits made during the period.
4. The number of cancelled checks.
5. The service charge—a fee taken by the bank for handling your checks and keeping a record of them.

Many banks divide this fee into two parts—a basic charge of $1 and then a charge of, say, ten cents a check.

Often, a bank will not levy a service charge if the customer keeps a sizable minimum balance (usually somewhere between $300 and $500) in the account at all times or has a savings account of a certain minimum (customarily in excess of $500 or $1000).

6. Beginning balance—the amount of money in the account at the start of the period.
7. Ending balance—the amount of money in the account at the end of the period.
8. The amount of each check handled, the date on which it was cashed, and the balance left in the account after the cashing.
9. The amount of each deposit made, the date on which it was made, and the account balance after it was made.

As soon as you receive your statement, you should compare its ending balance with the balance of money shown on the stub of your last check. Very often, the two figures won't be anywhere near matching. Perhaps you wrote some checks or made a deposit after the close of the statement period. Or perhaps certain checks written within the period didn't reach the bank in time to be included in the statement. Or perhaps you or the bank made some mathematical error along the way.

Whatever the case, you, of course, want to know exactly how much you have in the account at the moment. To help you find out, a special form comes along with the statement. It enables you to make a string of additions and subtractions that, involving your latest checks and deposits, end up comparing the amount shown in your checkbook with the amount that is actually in the account.

Hopefully, the two figures will be the same—or will, to use the bank's word, balance.

Using the form and the figures illustrated, let's see how this job of balancing works.

1. Begin by adding the statement's ending balance ($220.20) and the deposits made since the end of the period. Let's say that the deposits amount to $185.00 for a total of $405.20.
2. Next, list all your outstanding checks in the column at the right. These are checks written since the end of the period and those written within the period but not yet received by the bank. In this instance, they come to $150.45.
3. Now subtract this amount from the ending balance and deposit total of $405.20. The balance in your account is $254.75.
4. Suppose that you have a balance of $256.75 showing in your checkbook. Your work ends when you now subtract the service charge from that amount. In this instance, let's say that the service charge is $2. The balance becomes $254.75, the same as the balance in your account.

With the two figures matching, you can be sure of the amount of money you have in the bank. But suppose they don't balance. You now have more or less money (usually less, luck being what it is) on hand than you thought. There's an error somewhere and it will have to be found by going over the statement and your check stubs. Banks aren't beyond a mistake now and then, but the odds are that the error will be yours. Most likely, it will turn out to be a simple mistake in subtraction on some stub.

CHECKING ACCOUNT RECORD

		Number or date	Amount	
1. __220 | 20__ Ending balance		6/16	15	25
		6/17	10	00
2. __185 | 00__ Add deposits		6/17	5	10
		6/20	25	00
3. __405 | 20__ Subtotal		6/22	6	10
		6/22	2	30
4. __150 | 45__ Subtract outstanding checks		6/25	18	05
		6/28	30	00
5. __254 | 75__ Account balance		6/29	8	75
		6/30	29	90
6. __256 | 75__ Checkbook balance (before service charge)				
7. __2 | 00__ Enter service charge, if any, from front of statement. Deduct service charge from checkbook balance and enter new balance below				
8. __254 | 75__ Adjusted checkbook balance				
Account is balanced when lines 5 (account balance) and 8 (adjusted checkbook balance) agree.		**Total**	150	45

Your Savings Account

Want to set aside some money for a vacation? A new CB radio? A better apartment? Then a savings account is for you. Holding the money off to one side and keeping it out of easy reach, it's sort of an extra "strong box"— this time against the urge that we all have to spend the money in our pockets or checking accounts.

When you open a savings account, you'll receive a passbook, a small booklet which will serve as a record of your deposits and withdrawals. The bank will insure your account against loss due to theft, economic disaster, or bank mismanagement. This is required by federal law and all savings accounts are insured up to a maximum of $40,000.

If you wish, you may hold several savings accounts at one time, each for a purpose of its own. Each will be given a passbook, and each will be insured.

Since you're just getting started on your own, you probably won't have a lot to put aside. But don't let that bother you. In practically all banks, you can open what's called a *regular passbook* account for as little as a dollar to five dollars. Then you can add to it in any amount as you go along. With even a few dollars put in every payday or whenever possible, your money will grow at a surprising rate.

Incidentally, once you know the cozy feeling that comes with having a "nest egg" of your own, there's a chance you may get pretty ambitious and try to add a lot to it every payday. Big savings are great, but you'll be smarter to stick with just small amounts for the time being, increasing them a bit whenever you get a raise. A twenty-year-old San Francisco typist explains why:

"When you try to put too much away, it seems as if you're always running to the bank and breaking into your savings to pay for everyday expenses. It really gets discouraging and it can stop you from saving altogether."

She recalls, "I wanted to buy a stereo set and I tried to put aside $50 a month for it, but I got nowhere. So I settled for a more realistic figure—$5 a week. It took a while longer, but I finally got the set . . . The big thing is to save steadily and not to touch the money once you've put it away."

While you're saving, your account will help matters along and "manufacture" some extra money for you by earning interest. You can expect a regular passbook account to earn interest at a rate of between 5 percent and 5½ percent a year. You may take the interest out if you wish or you may leave it in the account.

It's a good idea to leave it in the account because all banks compound interest earnings. To see the value of this, let's say that you open an account with $2,400 left to you in a relative's will. And let's say that, in the first month, your money earns $10 in interest. At the start of the next month, if you leave the money alone, the interest will be computed on $2,410, earning you a slight bit more than would the original $2,400 by itself—for the sake of illustration, let's say $10.25.

At the start of the third month, the interest will be computed on $2,420.25, earning you still a greater amount. The process continues through the months and years, with the interest working on itself and bringing you greater and greater earnings.

Actually, though it illustrates the point, this example is an oversimplification of compounding. Most banks compound interest daily. This means that earned interest is added each day to your savings, with the next day's interest figured on that increased amount. By not touching the interest earnings, you can double the $2,400 in several years' time.

The regular passbook is only one type of savings account available at a bank. You can earn a greater amount of interest—over 6 percent a year—by taking out what is usually called a *bonus* or *premium* account. But there's a problem here. You must start with a larger amount of money (usually at least $500) and then not touch it for anywhere from three months to three years or more. The bank, which invests the money and makes a profit from it, makes these demands so that it can afford to pay the higher interest. If you break into the account too early, you'll be assessed a penalty. The penalty is required by federal law and involves a substantial loss in the interest earnings.

Bonus and other high-interest accounts are excellent means for building a nest egg. But they're best reserved for monies that you're pretty sure you won't be needing for an extended period. Since you've got to watch your pennies, it's wisest to start modestly and save a little at a time. Once you've saved a sizable amount, you can think about putting it into a bonus account.

You and Your Credit

It would be nice if you were rich enough to go through life paying for everything in full as you buy it. But the truth is that, sooner or later, you're not going to have the cash for something that you want or need and you're going to have to make your purchase on credit.

It's happened to just about everyone. For you, it may happen the first time you buy a car or furnish an apartment. When it does, you're going to run into that age-old document, the contract.

A contract is nothing more than an agreement made between two or more people—in your case, the agreement to buy something now and pay for it in a certain way later. But the contract covers all types of sales and trade for goods and services, and so it comes in a variety of forms. It may be made orally or in writing. It may use just a few words or cover many pages. Regardless of its length, it makes one overall demand on you: Once you enter into it, you must live up to its every provision. Should you violate it in any way, even accidentally, the other party has the right to demand that the problem be corrected. If necessary, he can go to court and demand that the contract be honored or that you pay him for any losses that he suffered.

Actually, even the smallest of everyday purchases, at the grocery store or the service station, are contracts. They usually don't cause any trouble. But, when you buy something expensive, there can be trouble with a capital T unless you're careful. You can really be on the spot if you agree to terms that you don't understand, if the other party is out to rip you off, or if either of you fails—accidentally or deliberately—to live up to everything in the contract. You can suffer financial losses that might hurt for months or years to come.

The Written Contract

There's only one way to avoid these problems—and that's to have the contract in writing and to understand every point in it. Then there's little or no chance of some misunderstanding causing a violation. And, if there should be trouble, you've got a written record of the agreement for everyone to see.

Any contract should contain all the details of the agreement. To make sure that the one you sign does, here are the main points you should look for when reading it over:

1. The names and addresses of everyone signing the contract should be given. There should also be mention of where the contract is being made.
2. The contract should explain very clearly what it's all about—say, the sale of a certain make and model car for so much money.
3. All costs should be included—not only the price of the car but also all other charges, taxes, and the amount being credited to you if you're trading in an old car.
4. If there are any special deals attached, they should be mentioned. For instance, suppose that you want special tires that aren't in stock and the dealer promises to get them for you at no additional cost. This should be stated.
5. There should be an explanation of how everyone is to handle an emergency. Let's say that the model car you want isn't on the showroom floor. You're going to need it

in a week for your new selling job. Though the dealer agrees to deliver it by this time, what's to happen if there's some delay? The two of you should decide on a course of action and then put it into the contract.

Once a contract is in writing, you should read it thoroughly *before* signing it. Don't become impatient with all the legal language and give up; legal terminology can be a drag, but, if you don't read the whole contract, you can be stuck with some condition that you don't like. If you don't understand any of the points, ask that they be explained. If you have any objections, voice them and have changes made. And if there are any blank spaces open for dates, amounts of money, and the such, have them filled in so that you're sure the right figures are used.

Only when you're completely satisfied should you sign. Once you've put your signature to the contract, you must honor its terms, no matter whether you like them or not.

From the very first days of your independence, you're likely to run into the written contract. As said earlier, it comes in many forms. Here now are some that you're bound to meet.

The Conditional Sales Contract

This contract, which is signed by millions of people daily, is most often used in the purchase of a car, furniture, or an expensive appliance such as a refrigerator, stove, or washer.

Rather than handing the salesman the full price, you make an initial part payment called the *down payment* or just the *down*. You then pay the remainder in equal portions over a given period of time. Each individual payment, which is usually made monthly, is known as an *installment*. While you're paying, you're allowed to take the merchandise home and use it.

You also pay interest. You're told the rate of interest and its dollar amount; the law requires that both be specified in the contract. The dollar amount is added to the purchase price and a part of it goes into each installment payment.

Let's put this all into an example. Suppose that you buy some furniture for $700 at 10 percent interest ($70). Your whole bill is $770 and you agree to pay it off over a period of twelve months. You make a down payment of $50, leaving $720. Your twelve installments will be $60 each.

The conditional sales contract is known by a variety of names—time payment plan, deferred payment plan, and installment sales or plans. Regardless of its name, it usually works this way:

1. Though you take the merchandise and use it as your own, the seller retains actual ownership until the final payment is made.
2. You and the seller agree on the conditions under which the merchandise is being purchased. These conditions include the number of installment payments, the amount of each, and the dates on which they're to be made.
3. Because the seller still owns the merchandise, you agree not to move it to a new location—especially one out-of-state—without first telling him and getting his permission.
4. The seller has the right to *repossess*—take back—the mer-

chandise if you fail to make your payments or violate the contract in some other way.

On this last point, repossession can be a pretty tricky business for both you and the seller. In general, though, you can reclaim the repossessed goods by catching up with your installments or paying everything off within a certain period of time. Perhaps the seller repossesses your car without giving you any notice; he then must hold the car for ten days before reselling it, and you may reclaim it during that time. Or he may notify you that he's coming to take it away. If so, he must tell you no less than twenty and no more than forty days ahead of repossession; you then have more time in which to act.

To repeat, repossession is a tricky business. If you're ever faced with it, you'll be wise to take your problem to a lawyer or a legal aid service so that you can find out exactly where you stand legally.

Credit Cards and Charge Accounts

Charge accounts issued by stores, and credit cards such as those issued by oil companies, Master Charge, and American Express are all contracts. You can use them and then pay them off completely each month or, as if they were conditional sales contracts, you can pay in monthly installments. Most oil companies, incidentally, expect you to pay your regular gas purchases in full each month, but permit you to put more expensive items—tires, batteries, and the such—on an installment basis.

Since charge accounts and credit cards are used repeatedly by the customer, the amount owing constantly varies. And so, if you're paying in installments, you'll find that the payments do not remain the same as they would for a single item. Rather, they fluctuate, with each installment being a percentage of the amount owing at the time the payment falls due.

Quite often, the installment comes to 5 percent of the amount outstanding. Should you, for instance, owe $400 one month, your charge will be $20. If you owe $460 the next month, your payment will jump to $23. Most charge accounts and credit cards require a minimum payment of $10 a month, meaning that, if you owe $90, you shoudn't expect your payment to be $4.50.

Charge accounts and credit cards usually do not charge interest as such. Rather, they impose what is called a *carrying charge*, a fee for handling your account. It's figured on a percentage of the amount owing, and, in most cases, comes out to a rate of 18 percent a year.

Applications for credit cards, such as Master Charge and American Express, can be obtained at many banks. Applications for oil company cards can, of course, be had at service stations. If you wish to open a charge account at a store, you'll need to drop by the credit department.

When filling out an application, you'll need to state the amount of your earnings and list several places where a check can be made on what kind of a credit risk you'll be. You may use your bank or some store where you already have credit for these references. You'll also be asked your age—and here you may run into trouble. Because a credit card and a charge account are contracts, you may find it impossible to obtain one if you haven't yet reached the age of majority.

If You're Underage

The reason for this restriction is that, in general, you're not permitted to enter into a contract on your own as a minor. If you do so and then decide not to live up to it, the other party won't be able to take you to court because the law holds that you don't have the maturity to meet the obligations that you took on. To protect the other party, the law says that an adult—a parent, a guardian, or a legally appointed guardian—must enter into the contract with you. The adult then becomes responsible for its terms and can be taken into court if you violate them.

As a minor, however, you are permitted to take on several specific types of contract by yourself. They then cannot be broken. Enlistment in the armed forces and the provisions of your driver's license are two such types.

Further—and this is especially important if you're living by yourself—you are usually responsible for any contract that secures for you what are called *necessaries*. These are the things required for everyday living—food, clothing, and shelter. If you buy a bag of groceries (remember, it's a contract), you're obliged to pay for them. If you're a certain age—say, seventeen—the courts will probably insist that you pay the rent (it, too, is a contract) on your apartment should you try not to. But, if you're much younger—perhaps thirteen or fourteen—your contract for rent usually won't be recognized by the judge.

As was said at the start, it would be nice if you could get through life paying cash for all your purchases. But, beginning salaries and inflation being what they are, the odds are that you're going to be in the same boat with the rest of 'us—you're going to buy things on credit, assuredly at times and possibly on a continuing basis. Try to use it wisely and as sparingly as possible and try never to violate the terms of any contract. The careless use of credit and the violation of a contract—either can damage your reputation, jeopardize your future purchases, and cost you both extra money and lost time in straightening things out.

7

You and Your Four Walls

"I guess the only thing you could call it was an adventure. I ran into all sorts of things I hadn't even thought about."

This is Cathy speaking about her search for an apartment of her own in the days before she left home three years ago. Apartment or house hunting is something that all young people must do sooner or later, and the chances are that you're going to share some of her experiences when you get to it.

How about the two of us looking together right now, just to see what might happen?

A Place of Your Own

You can get a line on the apartments, duplexes, and houses for rent in your area by visiting a real estate office that deals in rentals as well as sales, or by checking the classified ad section in the newspaper. In the classified section, rentals are listed according to whether they're furnished or unfurnished. Also listed are those which the present tenant wishes to share.

Suppose that you see this ad in the classified section:

> $175 A MO: 1 BR apt, w/w cpt, drps,
> frpl, AEK. No pets. Call mgr. at 568-3333.

The abbreviations, which can look like so much mumbo-jumbo if you don't know what they mean, are used to keep the ad within a small space and so cost the advertiser less. But, once you've learned to decipher them, you know what you're going to get for your $175—a one bedroom (BR) place, with wall-to-wall carpeting (w/w cpt), drapes (drps), and an all-electric kitchen (AEK).

It looks good. You call the manager for an appointment.

When you arrive, you may be in for a shock if you've got just enough for the rent payment. Most likely, the manager will say that certain additional costs will have to be met before you can have a key and move in. This isn't because he thinks you young and untrustworthy. Many—if not most—rentals call for all tenants to pay several moving-in charges.

Depending on the apartment, these charges come in different combinations. In general, though, you can expect to pay the following:

1. First month's rent
2. Security deposit
3. Cleaning deposit
4. Key deposit

The security deposit is meant to guarantee that you'll meet all the terms and conditions of the rental and that you won't wreck the place. The deposit is to be refunded when you move, if the apartment has not been damaged beyond what can be called "normal wear and tear" (faded paint, worn carpeting, a leaking faucet, and the such). Otherwise, the landlord may keep all or part of it to cover the costs of repairing such undue damage as broken windows, torn drapes, or cigarette burns in the carpeting.

Some landlords do not ask for a security deposit by name, but demand that the first and last month's rent be paid before moving in. The last month's rent, then, serves as the security deposit.

The cleaning and key deposits are exactly what they seem to be. The first is a charge for having the apartment cleaned before you and your furniture arrive. The second covers the cost of replacing your keys should you lose them. Incidentally, some landlords will let you sidestep the cleaning deposit if you take the unit "as is" and then clean it yourself.

There's no way here of saying exactly how much the several deposits will cost. They vary among apartments and depend much on the size and quality of the place. But a little figuring will give you a fair estimate.

Very often, the security deposit equals one month's rent —and certainly will if your landlord works on a first-and-last-month's-rent basis. If so, instead of $175 in rent, the moving-in payment jumps to $350. Cleaning deposits can run anywhere from $25 to over $100. For a place the size of yours, a figure of around $60 is a safe bet, bringing your costs to $410. Add another $2.50 to $5 for a key deposit and you're working with a total of around $415.

Once the initial bite is out of the way, there's still more to come. Now you're up against the question of how much beyond that $175 the apartment will cost you each month. To make certain that you won't run into too many unexpected expenses, you should take at least two steps.

First, ask the landlord about the services that he intends to provide. In most apartments, you'll have to pay for heat and electricity. But see if the landlord plans to handle the costs of garbage collection, water, and the TV antenna service. If so, you'll be a few dollars ahead of the game each month. If not—well, you know the answer.

Second, check the condition of the apartment and check into the extent of the landlord's responsibilities for repair and upkeep. The laws in all cities and states require that he take care of such headaches as faulty plumbing, falling roofs, and structural flaws. And practically all local sanitation and health regulations call for him to keep the plumbing, electricity, and gas lines in good working order. Also, he must maintain adequate means for fire protection, proper ventilation, and efficient garbage disposal.

But where does he stand on minor repairs? Who takes care of chipped plaster, loose hinges on doors, dripping faucets, windows that stick, and the such? Customarily, most are left to the tenant and, in many areas, they extend to painting the place. If the landlord intends to leave all minor repairs with you, then make sure that the unit is in reasonably sound shape before moving in. Otherwise, a string of small hammer-and-nail jobs may cost you a bundle in time and money.

Okay. You've looked the place over. It's what you want

and is within your budget. You tell the landlord that you'll take it. Now one more job remains before you can move in.

If the landlord is like most others, he'll nod and produce a formal-looking piece of paper for you to sign. It's a piece of paper that you'll be meeting time and again for as long as you rent rather than buy your living quarters—the lease.

Your Lease

A lease consists of a series of agreements into which you and the landlord enter. Chief among them are the ones on the amount of rent you'll pay and the length of time you'll live in the apartment. On signing the lease, you and the landlord promise to honor the agreements and he gives you the right to occupy the place. You become the *lessee*, and he is the *lessor*.

The lease is a contract and is as binding as any other. Should you or the landlord violate it in any way, the injured party can demand that it be fulfilled and can even sue the other in court for any monies lost.

As a contract, a lease may be made orally or in writing. Most landlords, though, will want it in writing, and, obviously, it's best for all concerned to have it that way. Of course, before ever signing it, be sure to check over all the agreements, making certain that you understand them. If the lease happens to be an oral one, you and the landlord should discuss the agreements to the point where no doubts are left about your responsibilities to each other.

Here now are some of the principal points that you'll find in any lease for living quarters.

The Amount of Rent

The payment of the rent is the first and greatest of your responsibilities to the landlord, and so its amount should be clearly stipulated.

In addition to the amount itself, a number of other points may be likewise stipulated. If they're not, you should ask about them. First, you'll want to know the exact date on which the rent falls due. Second, you should know how much of a *grace period*—a certain amount of extra time in which to pay without being assessed a penalty—you're to be given. And, third, you should know the penalties imposed for a late payment.

Many apartments allow a grace period of from five to thirty days and then demand a late charge of, say, $15, plus a charge of $1 or $2 for each day the rent remains unpaid beyond the grace period.

Incidentally, as a general rule of thumb, you usually have a thirty-day period in which to pay any bill without a penalty. But this won't apply if you sign a lease—or any other contract—that specifies a shorter grace period. By signing, you've agreed to the shorter period and you must stick to your word.

The Length of the Lease

The lease should leave no doubt as to its *term*—the length of time it is to run. Leases can run anywhere from several weeks to several years, and you should know definitely how long you're signing aboard for. It's a safe bet that an apartment lease will be for six months or a year. But make sure just the same.

The big thing to remember here is that, in signing the lease, you're committing yourself to a given number of rental payments. Unless otherwise agreed, you continue to be responsible for them even if you move out before the lease period is up. And, of course, before ever signing, you should make doubly sure that you have—or will earn— enough money to see you through the lease period.

Your lease will probably have blank spaces in it for the beginning and ending dates of your occupancy. Don't sign until the landlord fills them in with the right dates. If he's already written them in, double-check to be sure that he hasn't made some sort of error—accidentally or deliberately.

An accidental error, of course, can be corrected immediately, before signing. But if you see the error after you've signed and then discover that you're dealing with someone who has tricked you, you'll have to go to a lot of time and expense to prove his underhandedness before you can legally break the lease.

Your Responsibilities Under the Lease

Most leases include very specific agreements on what you may or may not do in or to the place. For instance, your lease may state that only two people can occupy the apartment; this, of course, doesn't apply to guests who stay overnight or for a few days, but protects the landlord against the possibility that you'll let an army of friends "crash" for extended periods. The lease may also say that you can't bring in pets or install a water bed. It may even prohibit you from hanging pictures by means of nails, requiring that you use adhesive hangers instead.

Should you fail to live up to any of these provisions, you become liable for certain penalties. They're stated along with the provisions and usually call for you to give up a part of your security deposit or pay extra monies. Some permit the landlord to break the lease and evict you.

One of your greatest responsibilities is to treat the rental carefully and, on your departure, to leave it in substantially the same shape as you found it. We've already said that you can lose all or a part of your security deposit by doing damage beyond normal "wear and tear." But there are three more points that also must be remembered.

First, you're just as likely to get into trouble if you try to improve the apartment by making a structural or design change. You may think the place will look better with picture windows in the living room and fancy wallpaper in the bedroom—and you may be right—but you may not go ahead with them on your own. You must first obtain the landlord's permission. If he says "okay," you may carry on according to whatever terms he sets. But if he shakes his head, forget it. It's his property and he has the right to look on any unauthorized change, even for the better, as damage.

The second point concerns just how much of your security deposit the landlord may keep for damage. He may not just look at some damage and take the entire deposit for it. He must show the actual cost of the damage and then take just enough to cover repair or replacement. If the damage adds up to more than the deposit, he has the right to go to court and ask that you be made to pay an additional amount.

The final point has to do with minor repairs. Though these jobs are usually left to the tenant, the landlord may prefer to do them himself, feeling that only then will the work be properly done. If so, be sure to tell him immediately whenever one becomes necessary. In this way, by not allowing some problem to worsen with time, you're doing your part to keep the rental in good condition.

But what if he fails to show up with his toolbox within a reasonable time? You may then do the job yourself or hire someone to do it, after which you can bill the landlord for your costs. In general, however, you may not deduct the costs from your rent. The law in most areas won't back you up if you do.

Subletting Your Apartment

When you sublet a place, you rent all or a part of it to another person. It's a step taken by many a young person who first rents by himself and then brings in a friend to share the costs when he finds that he really can't meet them on his own. Or by many a young person with a friend who "crashes" for a time and then asks to stay on in the spare bedroom.

You may, of course, sublet your apartment without telling the landlord if the lease gives you permission to do so. And you can do the same thing if the lease makes no mention of subletting at all. But many leases demand that you first get the landlord's permission.

This gives the landlord the chance to meet your friend and decide whether he or she is going to be a desirable tenant. Usually, however, the lease will state that the landlord can't refuse permission without proper grounds for doing so. He has to come up with a good reason for finding your friend undesirable.

When you sublet, your friend has all the rights that you do as a lessee; he can live there and come and go as he pleases. But he takes on none of your responsibilities under the lease. All these responsibilities—headed by the payment of the rent—stay with you. They can't be given to someone else without the landlord's permission. This is because your lease is a contract between just you and the landlord.

When Your Lease Ends

All leases are supposed to end automatically at the close of their runs. But don't count on this so far as yours is concerned. Check it over to see if there's an *automatic renewal* agreement in it. If so, it will call for you to notify the landlord ahead of time that you don't wish to stay on. Should you miss telling him, the lease will be automatically renewed for another run of the same length as the first.

You usually must notify the landlord either thirty or sixty days ahead of time. So, if you're planning to move at the end of the lease, be sure to remember the date of the notice and not let it slip by. Otherwise, you're stuck. You'll have to meet the rent payments until someone comes along and takes the apartment, or you'll have have to make some deal with the landlord. Either way, you're in for a lot of extra expense.

Even if you're planning to stay on, it's a good idea to get in touch with the landlord at notice time. This will give you a chance to learn if he plans to up the rent and then the chance to find a new place if you don't like the figure he has in mind.

Now for a problem that has bothered many a renter. Suppose that you're planning to leave but find that your new place isn't ready yet. And so you stay where you are after the lease has expired. You've now got what's called a *holdover tenancy*. How do you handle and then end it?

The answer should be right in your lease. The lease may say that the landlord will charge a day-to-day rent until you leave. Or it may say that he has the right to renew the lease for a complete new run. Either way—especially the last—can be pretty costly. Your best bet is to see if you can get some sort of inexpensive deal from the landlord or to leave your things with friends and stay with someone until your new place is ready.

Now for another problem: What can you do if you must end the lease before the close of its run? Actually, there's nothing to prevent you and the landlord from ending the lease at any time and for any reason. What you have to do is reach an agreement that is acceptable to both of you.

This agreement can take any number of forms. For instance, let's say that you've got a year's lease but that, with six months left to go, you win a scholarship at a distant university. You must leave in two weeks' time for the opening of class. The landlord may be softhearted or he may have a tenant ready to take your place. And so he wishes you well and lets you go without any extra charge. As soon as you leave, your lease ends.

But suppose that his new tenant won't be able to move in for a month or so. The landlord may demand that you pay the rent up to the day of the new tenant's arrival.

Or suppose there is no new tenant on the horizon. You may then have to make some settlement payment, or you may have to go on paying the rent until the lease ends or a new tenant is found. In this case, the landlord doesn't have to go out and look for someone new. He may not, however, deliberately keep from renting the apartment. If a good tenant shows up, the landlord may not turn him away just because it's easier to have you pay the rent. Once the new tenant has signed a lease for the apartment, yours ends.

The agreement that you and the landlord reach to end the lease ahead of time should be put into writing. Copies should be kept by you both.

8

You and Your Job

We've spent quite a bit of time talking about money. Now we come to a matter that could be the most important of the lot, the one about the thing you must have in the first place if you hope to get the money needed for a lasting independence—a job.

Many a young person first leaves home and then starts to hunt up a job, perhaps staying with a friend while doing so, perhaps getting along on some savings, or perhaps borrowing to scrape by. Though life on your own can be started this way, a young friend of mine, Gene, thinks that it's the hard way to do things and that the process should be reversed.

"Get the job first. Then think about leaving."

Why?

Gene's now twenty-seven and an assistant office manager in a Midwestern city. For the answer, he goes right back to his first days of independence nine years ago.

"I'd just graduated from high school and wasn't planning to go to college. All I wanted was to get out on my own and get a job. . . . So I set it up to stay with a buddy in his apartment while I went looking, and I thought everything was going to be great. . . .

"But it turned out just the opposite. . . . I bunked with him for three months and I had a few dollars set aside, but they ran out in about five weeks and he had to handle all the bills. . . . He didn't like that—no way—because he was just making ends meet himself. . . . Before I landed a job, I was even borrowing cigarette money from him. Now that was a real bummer. Like going to my father for a five when I was in my teens and had a date. . . . We're still friends and laugh about it now. But we didn't then. I think we were ready to start swinging at each other. I know I was. . . .

"And there was another thing. I looked for a job nonstop the whole time and I found out something strange. It's tough enough to get a job even when things are going good for you, but it's twice as tough when you're in trouble. . . . I don't know why but it seems that the more you need a job, the harder it is to land one. . . . Nothing seems to work out.

"I've talked with my boss about this and he says it's a common experience. He thinks it's because you get all tensed up and put out bad vibes and then nobody wants you around. You just don't have the self-assurance that makes you look like a winner to an employer. . . . I think he's right. I know he is when he says the best time to look for a job is when you've already got one."

In the end, things turned out fine for Gene. But he says it was a hard and embarrassing time. And so, when asked what he would do if he were back at square one, he answers quickly:

"No sweat. I'd stick around the house until I was really ready to go. I'd find a job first and then put as much money aside as I could. I'd probably be gritting my teeth the whole time and holding myself back from leaving too soon. . . . This isn't because I was having a bad time with my folks but because I'd be anxious to get started. But I'd be able to do it because I know things would be better at the other end. . . .

"I'd also make some financial arrangement with my folks. I'd want to pay them for my room and board. Then I wouldn't think I was sponging off them, and I'd also have the feeling of being at least partially independent. . . . And I'd feel pretty free to come and go as I pleased without always explaining like I used to do. . . . They probably wouldn't ask me to pay as much as I would for an apartment, and that would mean an added savings. . . . I'm sure all this would take just a few months."

I've talked to many young people who left home without a job as Gene did. They all agree that they had a difficult time and that his advice is sound and should be followed if at all possible. They also agree that, when the time comes to support yourself, you'll help your cause by asking three questions:

1. What sort of job will I need to get me by at the start?
2. What sort of job should I aim for in the future?
3. How should I go about getting a job, both the starting one and the one for the future?

Here are some ideas to help you with the answers.

A Starting Job

A first job is practically always a stepping-stone to something better and it may serve any number of purposes. Perhaps it's meant to tide you over while you get your bearings and decide what you want to do with your life. Perhaps it supports you while you take the training necessary for the career of your choice. Or perhaps, if you're already trained, it marks a start in your field.

No matter where you stand, the job needn't be a great one. In fact, it probably won't be, since you're a beginner and have little in the way of practical skill and experience to offer an employer. And so, while you'd certainly like to land the best first job possible, don't be upset if it turns out not to be very much. What counts is that it gets you started and enables you to live on your own.

There can be a problem, though, about a first job earning you enough to get by on. For the same reason that you really can't expect the job to be a great one, you can't expect to earn all the money in the world. Beginners usually aren't paid much because they must be trained on the job before they can begin to carry their own weight and because employers are reluctant to invest in a newcomer until he proves himself reliable and competent. Also, because you're a beginner, you may be starting with a small outfit that simply can't afford to pay you a great deal.

With this in mind, it would be a smart idea to check your budget once again before you go job hunting. Get your expenses down pat in your mind and know where and by how much they can be cut if necessary. This will keep you from making some mistakes when an employer does offer you work and tells you what the salary will be.

For instance, let's say that you're really disappointed with the salary figure, so disappointed that you turn the job down without thinking twice. You may be making a mistake and passing up a good offer—maybe the only offer that's going to be coming your way for a long time. But you're less likely to make this mistake if you already know how to cut your expenses to fit a smaller-than-hoped-for salary. Or if you've already made up your mind that you can do without something you were planning to buy. Or if you've thought about sharing expenses with a friend by renting an apartment together.

Or, even if the salary won't cover your expenses, no matter how you economize, you may be cheating yourself of a fine offer when a weekend job for the time being would provide all the additional money required to meet your expenses. Or perhaps you're going on to college and your parents have promised to help you along with an allowance; when combined with the allowance, the small salary may be just what you need. But you can only know these things if you know your budget and where it can be trimmed.

If the salary is uncomfortably low, don't forget to ask the employer how soon it will be before you can expect a raise. Many companies hire beginners at a small salary for a probationary period. The period usually runs from three to six months and is used to see if the newcomer is going to work out. Once the period is up, there's an increase in pay. And some companies gives raises periodically on the basis of merit. If you know your budget, you may be able to figure a way to get by until that first raise comes along.

Also, if the salary is really far too low, there's nothing to stop you from explaining your circumstances to the employer and seeing if he'd be willing to increase it a little. But be careful when you do this. Don't seem to be pushing. Make it clear that you need the money not for luxuries but necessities, and, above all, don't give him the idea that you think he's exploiting you by paying slave wages. In a nutshell, don't say anything to turn him off, but try to convince him of the truth of the matter—that you want and need the job and will do your best for him if hired.

If he says no, don't be surprised. Remember, he's going to be investing time and money in training you on the job, and his company may have a policy of paying beginners just so much and no more. If so, there's nothing he can do about it. And don't argue with him. Just think and then make the decision that seems wisest.

Aside from salary, there are some other things you should be thinking about as you go job hunting. For instance, let's say that you want a job that will support you while you attend college or a technical school. You'll, of course, try for one that will leave you sufficient time for class and homework, but be sure to avoid the temptation of taking a better paying one that has the wrong hours or that promises to interfere in some other way. No matter how much you'd like the job, remember that, if it cuts too much into your class and study time, it's going to hurt your grades and perhaps cause you to drop classes or decide to leave school for the time being.

These are all obvious dangers to the diploma you're seeking, with the last being the worst of the lot. Anyone who's dropped out of school temporarily, but just long enough to lose the habit of attending, will tell you how difficult it is to make yourself go back again.

There's also a danger that's not quite so obvious. It's great to have money of your own. Life starts to look very rosy indeed and it's easy to start thinking it will always be this way. Once that happens, you can get pretty lazy about school and even start thinking that you don't need it. This is an idea that should be resisted at all costs. The price you'll pay for it in the future will be great.

Another not-so-obvious danger: With money of your own, try not to start buying everything in sight. If you're at all prone to buying sprees, you can soon find yourself deep in debt and putting in a lot of overtime to catch up on your bills. Down the drain goes the time for study and, with it, your grades and even school itself.

Now a final note: Once you've enrolled, be sure to drop by the school placement office. Found on practically every college and technical school campus, it keeps a list of job openings for the students. Some are career jobs for after graduation and some are part-time jobs for during school and the summer. A few visits there—even just one—may find you exactly the first job you need.

A Job for the Future

Tom, who is now in his early thirties, is a regional sales director for a large manufacturer. Not the academic type, he didn't go on to college after high school but got a job as a clerk in a shoe store. Just when he was finding that he liked the work, he was drafted into the Army and sent to Vietnam. He likes to tell the following story about his return home.

"I got back in the late sixties. . . . I knew I wanted a selling job with the best company I could find. But I didn't have enough money to last me while I went looking. Hell, I didn't even have enough for some good clothes to go looking in. So I got the cheapest apartment I could find and a part-time job in a gas station. I pumped gas and saved up enough to buy a couple of good suits. Then I got dressed up, cleaned my fingernails, and started to knock on company doors, all the time going right on pumping gas at night. . . . It took me six months to land something. . . . I was lucky. . . . The job was with the company I'm still with."

Tom is a good example of someone who used a beginning job to support himself while hunting up the job he wanted for the future. And his experience is an example of the all-important advantage there is to knowing what you want for the future. He had a goal and so was able to go immediately after it—and to reach it in pretty short order. No time was lost in wandering about aimlessly after his return from Vietnam.

When we talk about the future, we're really talking about a career. So far as this subject is concerned, you're likely to be in any of three places at the moment. First, you may know exactly the kind of work you want to do and are training or preparing to train yourself for it on a beginning job or at a college or technical school. Or you could be already trained and ready to go. Or perhaps you've made no career choice as yet.

That third spot is a tough one to be in, a fact that you probably already know too well. You've had to put up with your relatives and older friends—and perhaps some younger ones, too—looking down their noses at you with that expression of "When are you going to start doing something? You can't sit around forever." You've had to go up the wall listening to your parents saying, "Why don't you try this or that?" Or to some aunt announcing to the family while she stares right at you, "My Jack is doing fine in law school. He just loves it."

Maybe you're fighting them all and telling yourself—and them—that your future and your life-style are none of their business. But, down deep inside, you may sense that they're right—that you really can't go on this way through all the years to come. That standing around and going nowhere can get pretty deadly after a time. That holding down some low-paying, dead-end job just because you can't think of anything better is enough to make you sick—and I mean *physically* sick. And that, sooner or later, you're going to have to get moving and pick something.

What a thought that last one is! The world is full of all kinds of careers and jobs that can be made into careers. But they're all mysteries. You don't know which you'd like or wouldn't like. Nor which might be dull on the surface but prove interesting once you've tried them—or vice versa. And you don't even know how to start finding out. So what are you to do?

A friend of mine who is a high school counselor has some answers. She spends much time with graduating students who are trying to figure out where to go next and she says:

"They almost invariably start by looking at the various careers. Then they try to choose one that they think they'll like and find interesting. And, of course, one that promises to pay the best.

"I think they're going about it all backwards. You're guessing when you try to pick a career this way. You won't know whether you really like it and find it interesting until you're actually at work in it—and, by then, you'll probably have put a lot of time and money into preparng yourself, and it will be too late to back out and try something else if you find you've made a mistake. . . . And, if you make your pick on the basis of money alone, you'll concentrate on only the best-known and glamour careers. You then run the risk of passing up the one that's best suited for you and that you'd be happiest with."

My friend advises everyone to turn the whole process upside-down. Don't start with a list of careers and then try to *fit yourself* to one by saying that it looks interesting or pays well. Rather, find out a few things about yourself— namely, your talents, your likes, and your past successes— and then pick the career that *fits you*. Then you can't help but be happy in it and good at it.

Finding out about yourself, however, takes some thought and time. You're going to be probing pretty deeply among a welter of ideas, impressions, and remembered experiences. To keep yourself from getting lost, my friend suggests the following three-step experiment. You'll need a few sheets of paper for it.

On the first sheet, make a list of all the things you *do best*. Ask yourself, for instance, am I good at writing, acting, speaking in public? Good at math, history, English, typing, languages? Am I good with my hands, and, if so, what sort of work do I do best with them—car repair, carpentry, welding, cabinetry? Don't be shy about admitting that you're good at something; assess your skills just as objectively as you can. False modesty can cause you to miss a fine—perhaps your best—talent.

Onto the second sheet goes a list of all the things you *like* to do best. How about asking yourself: Do I like to work on cars? Draw up plans of activities for school clubs? Repair electrical appliances? Do gardening work? Which school courses did I enjoy the most? And be sure not to overlook your hobbies and volunteer activities. Many a doctor and nurse began their careers as high school volunteer workers in a local hospital or convalescent home, and many a teacher as a Sunday school instructor or volunteer leader for a Boy or Girl Scout troop.

Now the third and last sheet. It's saved for the things you've done with the greatest success. For instance, were you the star of the school debating team? Or did you coach a children's soccer or baseball team that won a local championship? Or were you surprised when you did a really good job as sales clerk during the summer or over the weekends? Or surprised even more when you turned out to be a fine reporter, feature writer, or editor on the

school newspaper? And how about your school courses—
in which did you earn your best grades? Again—as on the
first sheet—no false modesty, please. Call your shots as you
see them. And don't overlook even the smallest success. It
could be the most significant of the lot.

Now it's time to compare the three lists. Before too long,
you should begin to see patterns of talents, likes, and past
successes that indicate one or more career possibilities. So
you've been successful as a part-time store clerk and like
to meet and talk with people; maybe you belong somewhere in sales. Or you're good at math, enjoy working in-
doors, and are the one that your club always seeks out
when it's time to organize an activity; how about a career
in business, perhaps as an office manager? Or perhaps
you're good at science, like to help people, and know more
about first aid than anyone else in your Scout troop; maybe
you belong in medicine—as a doctor, a nurse, a dental tech-
nician, or a hospital lab worker.

These are just three of the many possibilities that can
reveal themselves. The fact is, you'll probably see patterns
that indicate several career choices. If so, give them all
some thought so far as your likes and abilities are concerned and work them into an order of preference.

Once they're listed in order of preference, you're ready
for the next step—and that's to help yourself to a final decision by looking into the several careers and seeing the
work that each involves, the opportunities that each offers,
and the money that each pays. There are many books that
explain today's many occupations and most are available
in local libraries. The librarian will be more than happy to

help you find them. One of the best is the *Occupational Outlook Handbook,* which is published by the U.S. Department of Labor. It gives up-to-date information on more than 850 occupations, telling what the workers in each do, where in the country each is in greatest demand, and the training that each requires. It also tells you where you can seek out additional information about those that interest you the most.

And there's another benefit to be had from checking into the occupations. None of us knows *all* the types of jobs and careers that are to be found in the world. It's possible that you'll come upon one that you haven't even thought about and that suits you better than the ones on your list.

And there's yet another benefit. Your check may show that there are some dangers in your preferences. You may, for instance, discover that your number-one preference is in a field overcrowded at present and expected to remain so for many years to come, making your chances of breaking in pretty slim. You may decide to move on to your second choice, which is in an open field that needs workers. Or you may elect to go ahead with your first choice anyway and take your chances. The big thing is that, either way, you'll know what you're doing and won't be going at the future blind.

Now suppose that your list of talents, likes, and past successes doesn't clearly indicate any career choice. "Don't worry and don't be discouraged," my counselor friend says when discussing this possibility. "But," she adds, "it's more important than ever that you take the time to look into the various careers available. Knowing your likes, your skills, and your successes as you do, you're certain to find the job meant for you. But not unless you take the time to check."

Whether you've made any choices or not, she also suggests that you do more than check the books in the library. You'll be wise to seek advice from your high school or college counselor. A good counselor keeps posted on the careers and their opportunities and can do much to help you make a choice. And don't stay away from your school's "Career Day"; it could change your life. Also, don't overlook relatives, friends, and acquaintances who are in the fields of interest to you. They all can give you a good picture of what day-to-day life in an occupation is really like.

A Career: Five Do's and Don't's

My friend has one last bit of advice about a job for the future. She divides it into what she calls "the five do's and don't's" of going after a career:

1. *Do* attempt to decide on a career as soon as you can. The sooner you select your goal, the sooner you can start moving towards it. Make your choice carefully but make it efficiently, losing no more time than is necessary.
2. If you need to be trained, *do* start that training as soon as possible. Again, try not to lose precious time. Don't daydream about your career as being something for the future. Look on it as something you want today or, at the latest, tomorrow. Daydreams very rarely turn into realities.
3. Once you're taking your training—either at a school or on the job—*do* think of yourself as being in the career already. This will cause you to work and study more seriously and with greater interest. If the career remains a

daydream for the future, you'll run the great risk of "playing at" rather than working at your training.

4. *Don't* let someone talk you into a career. Your parents may think it will be great for you to be a doctor, a lawyer, or a certified public accountant. Or they may want you to go into the family business. Knowing you as they do, they may feel that you'll do well in fields such as these—and they may be right. But they also may be doing a little wishful thinking and hoping for the day when they can proudly say that you're in one of the prestige professions. So don't follow their advice *unless you really want to.* Make up your own mind, basing your decision on your knowledge of yourself. You may end up agreeing with them, but do so on your own and not because of any pressures they exert.

5. By the same token, *don't* pass up a career that you really like because you don't think it has enough prestige and won't make you as rich as some other. To put it bluntly, don't be a snob when making your choice. Pick a career that you really like and that, deep down inside, you know you're best suited for. You'll save yourself a lot of unhappiness later on.

Now let's take the next step. Let's say that you're trained and ready for a career job. Or that you want a job in which you can get the necessary training. Or one that will tide you over while you attend school. Whatever you want, the question is the same: "How do I go about getting myself hired?"

Finding a Job

It's natural to start looking for a job by asking your relatives, friends, and neighbors if they know of any available jobs. Quite often, they can be good sources, having heard of openings in their own companies or in those of business associates. And, being acquainted with you, they can recommend you to a prospective employer so that he looks at you with greater interest.

There are a couple of problems, however. Obviously, you may find that they know of nothing at all. Or they may only know of openings in businesses not of interest to you. And so you shouldn't lose any time in checking other sources.

Job Sources

1. *Classified want ads*: You've undoubtedly checked the newspaper want ads at one time or another and have seen that they list a wide variety of positions in all fields. But a newspaper isn't the only publication that carries want ads. You'll find them also in trade and professional journals. Here, of course, the jobs are limited to those within the fields covered by the journals.

Some professional and trade journals are available at the public library. If you have a friend in a field of mutual interest, you might ask if he has any journals that you might borrow.

2. *College and technical school placement centers*: We've already talked about these centers. But just let me mention them again as a reminder. They're excellent sources for both career jobs after graduation and part-time or summer jobs during the time you're attending class.

3. *State Employment Office*: Known now in some states

as the Department of Human Resources, this is one of your best bets. With offices in the major towns and cities, it has more job listings on hand than any other single source.

4. *The Chamber of Commerce*: Many Chambers keep a list of local job openings, and this is a source that's certainly worth a try. The location of your town's Chamber of Commerce is to be found in the telephone book.

5. *The U.S. Civil Service Commission*: This is the place to go if you're interested in a federal government job. It handles government placements here and abroad. An examination is required to qualify for these jobs. Job applications and information on the Commission and the examination are available at most post offices. Information may also be had by writing to the U.S. Civil Service Commission, Washington, D.C., 20415.

6. *Private employment agencies*: Most employment agencies specialize in just a few occupational areas. They're excellent if you're in search of secretarial, clerical, and general office work. Some may charge you a fee for registration and placement. Others will charge the company that hires you.

Looking for a Job

Once you've decided that you're going to find a job, waste no time in starting your search. There's an old saying that many jobs are obtained by "walking through the company door at just the right moment." A delay of even a day or an afternoon might cause you to miss that moment.

The following three points can help you use your time to the best advantage:

1. Make your search a full-time job in itself. Don't inquire at just one place per day. Try to go to at least one firm in the morning and one in the afternoon, calling early on both occasions so that you have ample time to fill out an application blank, take any tests that may be necessary, and perhaps be interviewed. Don't become discouraged at any time and take a little "vacation" of a day or so.

2. Before approaching a company, try to learn the best time to apply. Some like to take applications at certain hours or on certain days. A call to the personnel office can save you the time of a useless trip.

3. If you see an appealing job in the want ads or hear about one from a friend, call the employer immediately and ask to be interviewed as soon as possible, hopefully the next day. If he says "I can see you now," drop everything (except an already-scheduled interview) and get to him fast.

Your Resumé and Letter of Application

A resumé is a concisely written rundown of your job qualifications, aims, and previous employment. It is most often used when you're looking for a professional, technical, managerial, or administrative post, but can be prepared for any job. It may be sent by mail when you're inquiring about a job possibility or replying to a classified ad, or carried by hand when you're applying in person.

If you wish, you may write the resumé yourself. Actually, it's best to have it done by firms that specialize in preparing this "inventory of experience." They're listed in the telephone directory and their fees are quite reasonable. They'll interview you, write the resumé, and print up a number of copies so that you'll always have sufficient on hand.

Should you prepare the resumé yourself, you'll need to divide it into several sections:

1. *Personal data*: Your name, address, telephone number, date of birth, marital status, and dependents.
2. *Employment objective*: This section states the job or types of work you are seeking.
3. *Educational background*: Your college or, if you did not attend college, your high school; the dates of your graduation; the degrees earned; major and minor subjects related to the job you're seeking, plus any special studies, scholarships, and awards that may be of interest to the employer.
4. *Military experience* if any.
5. *Employment history*: This section, which is usually headed as "Experience," lists your previous employment. It may be prepared in either of two ways. You may list your employment job-by-job or you may categorize your jobs by function to demonstrate how they contributed to building the experience that will enable you to handle the position now being sought.
   In this latter method, suppose you're applying for the post of sales manager. You may list all your selling jobs together and explain the various types of sales experience they represent. This section would then be followed by a listing of those jobs or assignments in which you developed managerial skills.
   No matter which method is used, you should stress only

those jobs related to the one at hand, minimizing the others so as not to consume too much space or take too much of the employer's time.

If you're trying for your first job, the experience section is probably going to be on the brief side. But fill it out as best you can. You may list some of your better part-time jobs and those school activities that will show the employer that you are capable of handling a responsible job.

6. *Additional information*: Here, you may mention any skills that will add to your value as an employee. Should the company, for instance, maintain offices abroad or otherwise deal with other countries, it will be a good idea to list any foreign languages that you speak.

7. *References*: The names, addresses, telephone numbers, and positions of at least three people who are acquainted with your work and abilities should be listed here. If you've just graduated from school, the names of teachers or counselors may be given. If possible, you should have the permission of the people used as references.

So that you can see how the various elements are actually presented—and how work objectives and job experiences are concisely explained—here is a sample resumé:

John L. Davis (Date of resumé)
123 Hayes Drive Marital status: single
Woodford, California Date of birth: February 10, 1953
(zip code)
581-6656

EMPLOYMENT OBJECTIVE
Newspaper reporter, copy editor, editor

EDUCATION

State University, State City, California. BS degree, 1975

Major: Journalism. Minor: Political science. Extra courses: printing, beginning and advanced photography.

Extracurricular activities: Reporter and editor, *State University Tiger*, the school newspaper.

EXPERIENCE

1973-75: Summertime reporter for *Woodford Gazette*, Woodford, California. Covered police department and wrote feature articles. Also served as assistant photographer.

1975-77: Reporter, *The Hillman Times*, Hillman, California. Worked fulltime, covering City Hall and all city bodies, including city council, planning commission, and recreation commission.

ADDITIONAL INFORMATION

Since leaving State University, I have attended evening school to take additional studies in photography. I am capable of photographing all feature and news stories that I cover.

REFERENCES

Professor H. W. Bowen, Department Chairman, School of Journalism, State University, University City, California (zip code)

Paul Mackin, Editor and Publisher, *Woodford Gazette*, 15 Toyon Street, Woodford, California (zip code)

Mrs. Alice Golden, Publisher, *The Hillman Times*, 625 Almaden Street, Hillman, California (zip code)

In many instances, you'll need to write a letter of application to an employer, attaching your resumé to it. Perhaps the company is in a distant city, or perhaps, as is often the case, a want ad will direct all applications to be made by mail.

Since the letter of application is a self-introduction to a stranger, you'll want to give him the best impression possible. You should be brief, friendly but businesslike, and should state the job or type of position you're seeking. Your sentence structure, spelling, and punctuation, of course, must all be correct. Finally, the letter should be typed on a good quality paper—with no erasures allowed.

Here's a sample letter that may help when you're preparing your own:

Mr. Myron Cooper
Publisher, *Los Angeles Progress*
8950 Johnson Boulevard
Los Angeles, California (zip code)

Dear Mr. Cooper:

I have just learned from Professor H. W. Bowen of State University that you are expanding your staff to include another reporter who will specialize in writing human interest stories on local political figures. If you have not yet filled this position, I would appreciate the opportunity to be considered for it.

I have been interested in journalism since I was in high school. Now, after working full time for two years with *The Hillman Times*, which is published twice weekly, I would like to advance to a daily newspaper in a large metropolitan area and feel that I now have the experience to do so.

I am enclosing a resumé of my qualifications and background for your review. I would appreciate a personal interview with you so that my application can be discussed further.

Very truly yours,

John L. Davis

Enc.

The Job Interview

There's no need to stress how vital it is for you to "put your best foot forward" at the job interview. You're being granted a few minutes, sometimes as few as fifteen, to impress the employer not only with your job qualifications but with your personal qualifications as well—your willingness to work, your sense of responsibility, your integrity. To make the most of those minutes:

1. Show up on time. When an employer grants you an interview, jot down its time so there will be no embarrassing mistakes. Should you be unavoidably detained, perhaps by car trouble or some other emergency, call the employer and explain how late you'll be and why.

2. Dress neatly and conservatively. You and your generation may be accustomed to living in jeans, but they have no place in an office. Suits or a sports jacket and slacks are fine for men; a shirt and tie is preferred. Dresses or skirt suits are advised for women; pants suits are being accepted in more and more offices, but the employer may be one of the holdouts. Of course, man or woman, be clean and neatly groomed.

3. Review your qualifications beforehand, along with the answers to anticipated questions, so that you'll be able to speak as easily as possible. Speak modestly but confidently. You're sure to be a little nervous. Try to control it, but don't be upset if you fall over your tongue now and again. Employers expect and understand a certain amount of nervousness.

4. Let the employer ask most of the questions, so that he doesn't get the idea that you're interviewing *him* to see if the job is good enough. But don't hesitate to ask all the questions necessary to give you a clear picture of the job if he does offer it. A definite understanding of its duties and such matters as the opportunities for advancement will save the two of you future disappointment.

5. Listen carefully to what the employer says. His questions and explanations will likely indicate the type of person he wants. You'll then know better the points to stress in your answers. Or you may decide that the job's really not for you after all.

6. When questioned about your previous jobs or why you left them, answer honestly, but don't criticize your former employers or fellow employees. If you can't be tactful about them, he'll know that you won't be tactful about him.

7. If the employer has several jobs available, be flexible in discussing them. But give him a clear idea of your preferences. This will help him place you not only now but later when promotions and new openings come up.

8. Be ready to talk about the salary you'd like, but don't bring up the subject yourself. If the salary is open for

negotiation, be realistic in discussing the amount you think adequate. Often, the salaries for beginning workers are set at a given rate by company policy and leave no room for discussion.

9. The employer may want some time to make up his mind and may ask you to call for a decision or return for a second interview. Jot down the interview time and be sure to arrive on schedule. Should he say nothing about a future contact, ask him when you may call for a decision.

10. If the employer cannot hire you, ask if he knows of any other firms that may be in the market for someone with your skills and qualifications. Be sure to thank him for his time.

9

Your Independence—Today and Tomorrow

Your life of independence, as exciting as it promises to be and as exciting as indeed it will be, must still be lived just as your life today is lived. Day by day. With each day bringing its share of joys, disappointments, and problems.

Here now are four last topics, all intended to help you make each of those days as good as possible—first, for the good today, some ideas on how to pick and get along with a roommate if, in common with so many young people, you're starting your life in a shared apartment; second, for a better today and tomorrow, some thoughts on health; and, finally, for the best of tomorrows, some ideas on marriage and your future education.

You and Your Roommate

If you're like thousands of young people who want to save on the rent money, you'll share your first apartment with a friend. The fact that the two of you will be living together and sharing the same space (probably cramped) day after day makes the selection of just the right roommate all-important. If the two of you get along, all will be fine.

But if not—

I recently talked with several young friends about this matter, asking for their advice on how to choose a roommate and how to get along together. They've all shared living quarters with another and so the advice came quickly. It boiled itself down to four main points:

1. *Try to pick someone you like*: For Peggy, who is twenty-four and a secretary, this first point is the most important of the lot. "I'm sure that, if you like your roommate, you can overlook a lot of faults and personality traits that would otherwise get on your nerves something awful."

She recalls, "At the time I was planning to leave home, I had a school friend who wanted to get an apartment. She was okay, but not someone I really liked. But I agreed to take a place with her because I needed help with the rent—and, let's face it, because I wanted company—and there was no one else around. . . . It was a mistake. . . . At first, I was excited about the apartment and then I tried hard at being pleasant, but I just didn't like her and I'm sorry but she felt it. . . . I moved out in about six months. . . . We both would have been better off if I'd stayed home until I found someone I liked."

2. *Try to pick someone with similar likes and habits*: Both Peggy and Chuck, a college senior, agree that, while

a liking for your roommate is all-important, it sometimes isn't enough by itself. It helps to have some shared likes, traits, values, and habits. If you can get these things in combination with a liking for each other, "you're home free," Chuck says.

Like marriage, rooming together requires give-and-take and compromise on both sides, and so the two of you don't need to be carbon copies of each other. There is room for differences. But the differences shouldn't be extreme and shouldn't ever outweigh the similarities. What happens, for instance, when one roommate loves rock music played for hours at a time at full volume and the other can't stand it even when it's turned off? Or when one likes to study and the other likes to talk? Or when one has strict moral standards and the other keeps showing up with different bed partners?

Are answers really needed?

3. *Try to pick someone with a sense of responsibility*: This point means the most to Edith, a free-lance illustrator. She and a girlfriend agreed to split the expenses of an apartment down the middle. But the roommate proved to be a spendthrift and incapable of holding a job.

"We hadn't been in the place for two months before she was borrowing from me," Edith remembers. "Then, pretty soon I was buying all the groceries. And then it was the rent . . .

"Look, I'm a free-lance and don't earn a monthly salary and so I've got to be careful with my money. I just couldn't take it. At the end of the lease, I said that one of us had to go, and she said okay she'd go, and I had to hunt around for two months before finding someone else to come in with me."

4. *To get along best with a roommate, make some agreement as to how you're going to run the place*: Phil, who is the manager of a gas station, was the first to make this point, and it drew nods from everyone else. "It sounds strange, I know, but a house or an apartment is like a business. It won't run itself. You've got to run it and, to do that, you've got to know who's going to be responsible for doing what around the place, and when."

This can be done, Phil says, simply by sitting down with your roommate before you ever move in and taking a few minutes to split the household chores between yourselves.

"You can split them any way you want. One of you takes the cooking and the other sets the table and does the dishes. One cleans the living area and kitchen, and the other handles the bedrooms and bathrooms. One does the shopping, the other takes care of the outside area or washes the cars.

"If you want, you can trade jobs every week or month. Or if one of you really likes to cook and the other likes to water the plants, you can keep the same job permanently. . . .

"As I say, it doesn't matter *how* you do it. What matters is that you *do* it. Otherwise, you can have a real mess on your hands. Or one person can end up doing all the work, and that's bad—especially if it's you."

Phil adds that he and his roommate have also set times when each can bring someone in and have the place to himself; the other goes out to the movies, to the library, or on a date. Each roommate has one night a week for this "privacy time," as they call it. It ends at midnight so that the other isn't wandering around or sitting out in his car until all hours.

Your Invaluable Health

We all hope that we can go for years, even a lifetime, without a serious illness or injury. But it's just a hope. Illness and injury are ever-present dangers that become hard realities all too often for all too many people.

Even when only moderately serious, illness and injury can be costly—costly not only in terms of the money spent to be rid of them but costly in the terms of the money lost through lost working time. Further, in today's inflationary period, the price tag for the simplest medical care is especially high, and there is no indication and no reason to believe that it will do anything but become more so as time goes by.

Health and Disability Insurance

You can—and would be foolhardy not to—protect yourself against these costs by taking out a health insurance plan. You may do so on your own, at work, or perhaps through your union, covering not only yourself but your wife and children. Plans purchased at work or through a union are less expensive than privately held ones because the carrier, covering the workers as a group, can issue the insurance at a lower per-person premium and still turn a profit. Also, some employers and unions pay a portion or all of your premium.

A wide variety of health insurance plans are available today. Some pay a percentage of doctor, hospital, laboratory, and drug costs. Some pay all hospital costs and a percentage of the others. Some provide additional monies for the costliest of illnesses, such as cancer and heart disease. Most, among them the Blue Cross and Blue Shield plans, allow you to use your own doctor and the hospital of your choice; on the other hand, the Kaiser plan provides you with its own doctors, hospitals, clinics, and laboratories.

Though a good health insurance plan will protect you against the costs of illness and injury, one problem remains. What about the earnings you'll lose if you're laid up beyond the amount of sick leave you've collected at work?

You have several safeguards in this area. First, you may take out disability insurance at work or perhaps through your union. Obtained at a very low cost—often for as little as $4 or $5 a month—it pays you a percentage of your salary while you're off the job. It does not, however, go into effect on the day you fall ill or are injured. Rather, you usually begin collecting after thirty days or so, or after your sick leave has been used. The insurance covers you for illnesses and injuries suffered at or away from work.

Most, if not all, states require that an employer protect his people against lost wages by providing them with what is generally called *workman's compensation* insurance. It covers you for a percentage of the earnings lost due to illness or injury suffered while on the job and is effective right from the first day of the illness or injury. The employer usually pays the entire premium for this insurance.

Even if you're covered by workman's compensation, you'll be wise to take out disability insurance. One will cover you for on-the-job illnesses and injuries, the other for those suffered while you're away from work.

If you pay Social Security, you are entitled to certain salary-replacement benefits under its Old Age, Survivors, and Disability Insurance program. These benefits, however, are customarily paid only if you're incapacitated for an exceptionally long period—for more than a year, say, or for a lifetime.

Finding Medical Help and a Doctor

Now let's talk about a health problem that can be really troublesome for the young person who settles in a new and strange town or city. It can all be summed up in just one simple question: "Where can I get medical help if I need it?"

A doctor friend of mine has a few suggestions:

"On arriving in town, check right away for the location of the nearest hospital or clinic. There's nothing worse than having to hunt up a doctor or a hospital in the phone book when you've got a high fever or are standing there looking at a cut hand that needs stitching.

"If you can't get out of the house on your own or can't be moved without worsening your condition—maybe you're suffering an acute attack of appendicitis or have just fallen off a ladder and broken your leg—then the best thing you can do is call the police or fire department.

They'll get to you quickly and take over, calling an ambulance and doing whatever else is necessary. Many fire departments have emergency and rescue squads. They come in their own ambulance and are able to give first aid for even the most serious of problems.

"It's a good idea to list the numbers of your hospital and your fire and police departments alongside your telephone book. And, of course, you should keep a first aid kit in the house to take care of all those cuts, bruises, and scrapes that come along now and again.

"Finally, once you're settled in town, you should try to find a doctor who can take care of you on a continuing basis, just as your family doctor did back home. Then, when you need a checkup or when anything goes wrong, you'll have someone definite to turn to."

But just how do you find a doctor for yourself in a strange town?

Aside from picking a doctor at random from the phone book, there are three ways. First, why not talk to your family doctor at home before leaving? He himself or one of his colleagues may be able to recommend someone in your new town. Second, you can ask the public health agencies in your new town for their suggestions; they're well acquainted with the local doctors and will probably be able to name several who will best fit your needs and your pocketbook. Finally, your new friends and fellow employees—and any relatives that you may have in town—are always good sources for suggestions.

Once you've collected several names, there's nothing to stop you from visiting with each of the doctors, telling each that you're thinking about using his services, inquiring after his fees and policies (does he make house calls, for instance, and who replaces him while he's on vacation?), and getting to know him personally. On the basis of these interviews, which shouldn't cost you anything, you can then pick the one you think best meets your likes and your needs.

For the Future: Marriage

No one needs to tell you how serious marriage is and that it demands unselfishness and a deep sense of responsibility in both partners. I'm not going to preach to you about the wisdom of finding just the right partner and approaching the altar with care so that a happy lifetime together—and not divorce, annulment, or separation—will lie ahead. You already know all this for yourself.

But there are two problems that must be mentioned. Both are widespread, one having to do with your very understandable desire to leave home, and the other with your age.

Marriage and Freedom

The first problem takes shape when young people realize that, once they're legally married, they can leave home freely and not be forced to return again. With this in mind, many—some unconsciously and some quite consciously— come to see marriage not only as a union with a loved one but also as a convenient means for securing their freedom. It's an idea that almost always ends in disaster.

Kathy, who is twenty-three, divorced, and the mother of two little girls, saw marriage this way. She says bluntly:

"I don't care how anxious you are to get out of the house. Don't use marriage as the way for leaving. I did, when I was eighteen, and it doesn't work."

She runs a hand through her hair as she starts to explain. "I was pretty mixed up at the time. . . . My parents were the possessive type and we'd been having some pretty terrible fights because I was starting to get restless and was saying I wanted to rent an apartment. . . . They just couldn't understand why I wanted to leave a perfectly nice home . . . And me, I just didn't have the nerve to walk out and hurt their feelings. . . .

"Then I met my husband. He was in his twenties and nice and I think I loved him. At least, I was attracted to him physically. . . . I was very happy when he asked me to marry him, but the thing I kept thinking was—this is it. Now they can't say a thing. . . . It's an awful thing to say, but that's what I was happiest about. . . . Not the wedding or anything like that. . . . But that I was going to get away.

"Well, it was all a mistake. We stayed together for three years and then there was no use in going on. . . . I guess I loved him but just not enough . . . And I guess I wasn't ready for marriage. . . . I had wanted a new life so bad, but there I was in another house, loaded with responsibilities and cooking and cleaning and tied down just as much as I had been before—and more so when I had babies to care for."

There's a toss of her head as if she's trying to pull all her thoughts together. "I'm not saying that some people aren't ready for marriage when they're in their teens. All I'm saying is, don't use it as a way of breaking free. . . . Maybe the thought can't help but cross your mind when somebody proposes to you. It's okay if it does, just so long as the desire to get away is a secondary thing. The desire to marry has got to be the first, the main, thing. . . . If it's not, no marriage is going to work."

And now there's a long inward look.

The Age for Marriage

The second problem concerns young people who are yet below the legal age set for marriage. It puts in an appearance when, eager as they are to be away from home and on their own, they fool someone into marrying them. Once they've said "I do," they think that they're safe and that no one can now tear them apart.

They're quite mistaken. They can run into difficulties that will see them back in their individual homes again, with their short-lived freedom together a thing of the past. But, before looking at these difficulties, we really should get the legal age for marriage straight.

That age is set by state law and varies all across the country. Basically, though, it is divided into two categories. First, you may marry at one age *without* your parents' consent. Second, at a slightly younger age, you may marry *with* their consent. If you are below this latter age, you may not marry at all, even if you have parental permission.

There was a time when, in all but a handful of states, a

man had to be twenty-one before he could marry without parental consent, and a woman had to be eighteen. But now that the federal government has set the voting age at eighteen, the states have begun to lower the male age for marriage without parental consent to the same level so that the two ages will correspond and cause less confusion. But, contrary to the belief of many a young person, the states have not been required by law to make the adjustment. The decision to adjust is strictly up to each state and, for reasons of their own, many states have not yet made the adjustment—and may not do so for years to come, if ever.

Prior to the first lowerings of the without-consent age, thirty-one states and the District of Columbia permitted a man to marry at eighteen with parental permission; in the remaining states, the ages ran from fourteen through seventeen. Most states permitted a woman to marry at sixteen with consent; in the others, she could be as young as twelve or as old as eighteen.

The adjustment of the without-consent age has caused a corresponding adjustment in the with-consent age. The chart below, incorporating both the new with- and without-consent ages, shows the levels that were in effect at the end of 1976. Since it is possible that your state has adjusted its levels since then, the chart is intended as general information only. The latest word on your state's age requirements can be obtained from the marriage license bureau in your county.

State	Without Consent		With Consent	
	Male	Female	Male	Female
Alabama	21	18	17	14
Alaska	19	18	18	16
Arizona	18	18	16	16
Arkansas	18	18	17	16
California	18	18	—	—
Colorado	18	18	16	16
Connecticut	18	18	16	16
Delaware	18	18	—	16
District of Columbia	21	18	18	16
Florida	21	21	18	16
Georgia	18	18	18	16
Hawaii	18	18	16	16
Idaho	18	18	16	16
Illinois°	18	18	—	15
Indiana	18	18	17	17
Iowa°	18	18	16	16
Kansas°	18	18	—	—
Kentucky	18	18	18	16
Louisiana	18	18	18	16
Maine	18	18	16	18
Maryland	21	18	18	16
Massachusetts	18	18	—	—
Michigan	18	18	—	16
Minnesota	18	18	—	16
Mississippi	21	21	17	15
Missouri	18	18	15	15
Montana	18	18	—	—
Nebraska	18	18	18	16
Nevada	21	18	18	16
New Hampshire°	18	18	14	13
New Jersey	18	18	—	16
New Mexico	21	21	16	16
New York	18	18	16	14
North Carolina	18	18	16	16
North Dakota	18	18	—	15

State	Without Consent		With Consent	
	Male	Female	Male	Female
Ohio	18	18	18	16
Oklahoma	18	18	16	16
Oregon*	18	18	18	15
Pennsylvania	18	18	16	16
Rhode Island	18	18	18	16
South Carolina	18	18	16	14
South Dakota	18	18	18	16
Tennessee	21	21	16	16
Texas	18	18	16	16
Utah	21	18	16	14
Vermont	18	18	18	16
Virginia	18	18	16	16
Washington	18	18	17	17
West Virginia	18	18	18	16
Wisconsin	18	18	18	16
Wyoming	21	21	18	16

Blank spaces appear at points in the chart. They mean that the state either has no minimum with-consent age or is in the process of deciding on one. If no age is listed for your state, a check with your local marriage license bureau will let you know where you stand. An asterisk (*) indicates that your state requires not only parental consent for your marriage but court approval as well.

In general, even if you have their permission, you may not marry when you're below the age requiring the parents' consent. There are exceptions to this rule, however, in a few states. In some, the marriage can take place with court permission. In others, marriages are allowed if the couples have or are expecting a child. The matter is left up to the court, and the judge will usually approve the marriage only if it seems absolutely necessary for the welfare of the couple and the child. He may refuse permission if one of the partners has a poor police record or a venereal disease, or if there is doubt about who the father actually is.

Now let's say that you're underage but still manage to marry inside your state without getting the necessary parental permission. Somehow, you lie your way to a license and then fool a minister or a justice of the peace into performing the ceremony. What are the problems you can run into?

For openers, don't think you're safe from your parents just because you've said "I do" and then spent the night with your spouse. You're not legally married and so they still have control over you. They may throw up their hands and say, "All right, have it your way." But they may, if they wish, have the marriage annulled—declared null and void, as though it never existed. They not only have the right to do this but they have the right to do it over your objections. They can go right ahead, even if you fight them every inch of the way and show everyone how well the two of you are doing.

There's another danger. This one comes from your spouse. Suppose that, after the excitement of the wedding has passed, he or she suddenly wants out. You can be abruptly left high and dry because, until the without-consent age is reached, an annulment is very easy for a young person to obtain. Once that age is reached, a firm restriction comes into play. The spouse must show that the two of you have not lived together as man and wife since then. If this can't be proved, an annulment becomes so difficult (in fact, almost impossible) to secure that the spouse usually must turn to divorce or separation instead.

An annulment can be especially hard on a young girl. In a divorce or separation, the wife is usually entitled to some support money from her husband—sometimes for herself and almost always for the children. But, depending on the laws of her state, she may not be able to get any support for herself when the marriage is annulled. The husband, however, will usually be expected to support the children if there are any.

In either case—whether a fed-up spouse or your parents call for an annulment—there goes your dream for an independent life together. You're back home again—and with everyone keeping a particularly wary eye on you.

And here's yet another problem. A look at the age requirements can be pretty frustrating. You may see that, in your own state, you're not old enough to marry without parental consent but that you're quite old enough to do so in a neighboring state. So you and your loved one head across the border. But what happens when you return? Is your marriage considered legal in your home state?

The answer depends on the laws of your home state. If you're unlucky enough to live in one of a few states, you're in trouble. They hold that, to be legal, a marriage must be in accordance with the laws of *both* the outside state and the home state. Since it was against the law to marry at home without permission, the marriage, though perfectly legal across the border, won't be recognized upon your return. You'll either have to remain across the border—trying to find a job and start a new life—or return to hear that you're still under your parents' control and can be forced back into their home again.

Or you might be luckier and live in one of the states whose laws say that a marriage which is legally performed elsewhere becomes legal back home. But watch out. This is just a general law and there can be exceptions to it. For instance, your state may say that the marriage isn't legal because you deliberately ran away to avoid the age requirement.

If you're very lucky, you may live in a state that says the marriage is legal even if you took off to avoid the age requirements. There are a few states that hold this view. For them, the fact that the marriage was legal where performed overrides all other circumstances.

If you're thinking that you can get around your state's law requirements by going to another state, please be sure that you check the law before you leave. Take care that you're not making a mistake.

In fact, no matter whether you're of age or not, and no matter whether you need parental consent or not, take care when thinking about marriage. I know that I promised not to preach—but marriage is something for all your future. As such, it's a step that deserves much thought before it is taken.

For the Future: Education

Unlike marriage, going off to college can be—and often is—used as a convenient means for leaving home. It's an excellent and pretty painless avenue to freedom, no matter what your situation at home. All you need do is take a suggestion from Ellen, who is now teaching kindergarten in northern California.

"My parents weren't actually possessive . . . but still— well, they just didn't like the idea of my going off on my own. . . . I think they were worried about M-E-N chasing after me, which was pretty silly because I'd been chased by some real experts in my hometown. . . . And I guess that my mother still thought of me as her "little girl." . . . Anyway, it made it pretty hard for me to even think about talking to them about leaving. . . .

"But," and here she grins, "it just so happened that the best college for teachers was about two hundred miles away. . . . Or shall we say that I convinced them it was. . . . Now who can argue when you want to go to where you can get the best education possible? . . . My dad drove me up there in the fall and didn't say a thing."

Ellen's logic is perfect. Practically all parents want the best for their children. And all parents can't help but be happy when the kids show the good sense to want the finest education possible for themselves. And so even the most possessive Mom and Dad aren't likely to put up much of a fight when the best or the only college available to you happens to be clear across the state or in some other state. Away you go, leaving a sense of pride and not anger behind.

There can be a couple of problems, though, if your parents are paying all or a major part of your tuition and expenses. You may be expected to call or write home more often than would otherwise be the case. Or you may have to give an accounting of how you're doing in class and how you're spending your money. But these are minor headaches and, though they may get on your nerves from time to time, they're a small price to pay for being out on your own.

And you may sense that you're not really independent. The fact is, you're not—not, really—if you're underage or having your tuition and expenses paid for you. But, again, this is a small price to pay. At the least, you're away and out of the house. At the least, you're making your own everyday decisions. And, at the least, you're giving your folks the chance to get used to not having you around so that there'll be no trouble in the future when your day of complete independence comes.

You're one of the lucky ones if you're getting parental help for your college education. But what if you aren't so fortunate? What if you left home the day after high school graduation, took some job, and didn't go on to college? Or what if you went out and got a job because your parents couldn't afford to send you to college? Or what if you got so fed up with things that you dropped out of class and took off on your own before you earned even a high school diploma?

It's possible that your independence and your future are looking pretty sour at the moment. Perhaps you're stuck in a dead-end job because all the good jobs require a better education than you've got. Perhaps you've decided on a career and are up against the fact that it's going to take some training to get you ready for it. One way or the other, to give you the best future possible, you're going to have to get some more education, either by going to college or a trade school or by finishing off the work necessary for your high school diploma.

Here are some ideas to help you along your way.

If You're Going to College

As you know if you've already made inquiries, the work necessary to obtain a college degree requires much time and expense. But the rewards at the end, in terms of both the knowledge you acquire and the increased earnings it can bring, make the effort more than worthwhile.

You can attend college full time or part time. Of the two, the former is preferable and should certainly be your choice if your parents have said they'll pay all or a major share of your expenses. You'll win your degree all the sooner and, as always happens when you're giving most of your time to a project, you'll have a sense of forward momentum on your side.

The full-time route is a difficult one, though, if you're paying your own way. Let's face it, it can be tough to attend every night after working all day—or vice versa. And so it may be wiser for you to attend part-time. You'll be a year or so longer at the job, but many successful people have done it this way.

No matter how you choose, just be sure to do two things, especially if you're paying your own way. First, set your diploma as a goal that you won't stop trying to reach even if the road gets pretty difficult and tiring. And, if you're ever tempted to quit for a semester or so, give yourself a little kick and keep going. Once you've stopped, there's the danger of losing momentum and not getting back into gear again.

Practically every college has scholarship and aid offices on campus. You might check with those at your intended school to see if they can provide you with some financial aid. And don't forget to check with the placement office.

Junior Colleges

Depending on your educational aims, it might be a good idea to start your university work at a junior college—or, as it is often called, the community college. It offers the first two years of college studies. At the end of—or during— that time, you may transfer to a university or senior college (four-year) and complete your degree there.

Also, if you're planning on going into a trade or any type of secretarial, clerical, or office work, the junior college may be the place for you. Upon completion of two years' work, you'll receive an Associate of Arts degree. It's not a full college degree, but it is usually considered more valuable than a high school diploma when the time comes to apply for a job.

Many junior colleges are part of the local public school system and so may be attended free or for a relatively small fee. In most cases, you must pay for your books and supplies.

Technical and Correspondence Schools

High school diplomas and those for the trades (including office occupations) and a certain few professions can be obtained through technical and correspondence schools.

There are many excellent technical and correspondence schools. But the world also has its shares of ones that are rip-offs. Unless you or some friends have personal knowledge of your intended school, you'll be wise to investigate it thoroughly before ever enrolling. In particular, look into any claims that it makes about placing its students in jobs after graduation.

You can usually check out a technical or correspondence school by writing to the Better Business Bureau or Consumer Advocacy office in the city in which the school is located.

One caution about correspondence schools needs always to be kept in mind. They ask that tuition be paid in advance or in installments, sometimes for a semester, a year, or the full course. Other schools do the same thing, *but* correspondence courses require a great deal of self-discipline to complete. In practically all cases, the tuition is not refundable should you decide not to finish the work or simply quit.

Incidentally, if you'd like to do something such as clerical, mechanical, or food service work, you should check to see if there's a regional Occupational and Vocational Training program in your area. Publicly financed, O and V programs are to be found all across the country and are offered free or at very little cost. Information can be obtained at the main office of your school district or at the State Department of Employment.

That All-Important High School Diploma

Since most employers now require a high school diploma as a prerequisite for all but the most menial of employment, you can be in a real bind as a high school drop-out when the time comes to find a job. The bind worsens with the news that many technical schools also demand the diploma for entry and that some unions want it for admission into their apprenticeship programs. And it gets as bad as can be when you think about going back to school and having to sit with a bunch of young kids for anything from a semester to two years.

Actually, a second look will show that the situation isn't all that bleak. First, you may not need to go back to your old classroom. Many school districts offer high school courses under their adult education program. These courses can often be taken either during the day or at night. Day classes are usually presented in specially assigned quarters away from the regular students. Often, the adult program has a campus all its own.

Now for the matter of time. There may be a way of cutting a corner here.

As a shortcut to a diploma, many states allow former students to take the *General Education Development* (G.E.D.) test at age eighteen or older. The test, which is also used by the military for placement, covers the various areas of high school study. Should you take the test and pass its several parts, you'll receive a certificate saying that you hold the equivalent to a secondary school education. Should you pass just some part, you'll need to attend certain classes—but *only in those areas where you failed*. It's possible that you may have to take only one or two courses.

Information on the G.E.D. test can be obtained from your local school district office.

So things might not be so bad after all. And if they do prove to be on the difficult side, try to remember what was said at the first about a college education being more than worth all the time and effort. The very same thing applies to your high school diploma.

At this point, there's only one thing left to say—no matter your education, no matter your plans for the future, no matter whether you're just now finding your independence or coming up to it in the next days, weeks, or months:

To you all, good luck and happiness.

The Author

EDWARD F. DOLAN, JR., a native Californian who now lives just north of San Francisco, was raised in Los Angeles. After serving in the 101st Airborne Division during World War II, he worked as a teacher and then as a newspaperman and magazine editor.

He began writing books in 1958 and his first, *Pasteur and the Invisible Giants*, was published by Dodd, Mead. Since then, he has written more than thirty books for both young people and adults. He has also written numerous magazine short stories and articles.

Mr. Dolan and his wife, Rose, have two children, both grown and married.